D0030671

THE CURE FOR SOUL FATIGUE

Spiritual healing for the worn out, stressed out, and burned out.

Karl Haffner

Pacific Press® Publishing Association
Nampa, Idaho
Oshawa, Ontario, Canada

MVFOL

Edited by Tim Lale
Designed by Dennis Ferree
Cover photo/art by Romilly Lockyer / IMAGE BANK

Copyright © 2001 by
Pacific Press® Publishing Association
Printed in United States of America
All Rights Reserved

Library of Congress Cataloging-in-Publication Data
Haffner, Karl, 1961-
    The cure for soul fatigue : spiritual healing for the worn out, stressed
out, and burned out / Karl Haffner.
        p. cm.
    ISBN: 0-8163-1840-9
    1. Christian life—Seventh-day Adventist authors. 2. Spiritual heal-
ing. I. Title.

    BV4501.3 .H34 2001
    248.4'86732—dc21   00-054341

01 02 03 04 05 • 5 4 3 2 1

All Bible texts quoted in this book are taken from NIV, unless otherwise noted.

NEW INTERNATIONAL VERSION (NIV)
Scriptures quoted from NIV are from the Holy Bible, New International Version, copyright © 1973, 1978, 1984 by the International Bible Society. Used by permission of Zondervan Bible Publishers.

NEW REVISED STANDARD VERSION (NRSV)
Scriptures quoted from NRSV are from the New Revised Standard Version of the Bible, copyright © 1989 by the Division of Christian Education of the National Council of the Churches of Christ in the U.S.A. Used by permission. All rights reserved.

NEW ENGLISH BIBLE (NEB)
Scriptures quoted from NEB are from the New English Bible, copyright © the Lockman Foundation 1960, 1968, 1975, 1977. Used by permission.

LIVING BIBLE (TLB)
Scriptures quoted from TLB are from *The Living Bible*, copyright © 1971 by Tyndale House Publishers, Wheaton, IL. Used by permission.

NEW CENTURY VERSION (NCV)
Scriptures quoted from The Youth Bible, New Century Version, copyright © 1991 by Word Publishing, Dallas, Texas 75039. Used by permission.

NEW LIVING TRANSLATION (NLT)
Scripture quotations marked (NLT) are taken from the *Holy Bible,* New Living Translation, copyright © 1996. Used by permission of Tyndale House Publishers, Inc., Wheaton, Illinois 60189. All rights reserved.

PHILLIPS
Scriptures quoted from Phillips are from the New Testament in Modern English, Revised Edition, copyright © 1958, 1960, 1972 by J.B. Phillips. Used by permission of Macmillan Publishing Co., Inc., New York.

Dedicated to Teryl Monson

In loving memory of Paul Monson . . .
always a recharge to my soul

Special thanks to . . .

Tim Lale—a gifted editor with the patience of Job! I appreciate your long-suffering spirit.

Marc, Paige, and Sue—some of my most cherished childhood friends who remain a great inspiration to me.

Jerry and Lisa—true buddies.

Bob, Connie and Dana Melashenko—some of the most encouraging folk I know.

Henning, Troy, Leslie, John, Kraig, Bruce, Debbie, and Jan—my pastoral colleagues at the College Church who make work feel like Christmas every day.

Cathy, David, Paul, and Fae—for allowing me to share your inspiring story.

My family, Cherié, Lindsey, and Claire—a blessing beyond words.

Contents

Dripping the Soul Dry

Drip. Drip. Drip. Drip.

It's three o'clock in the morning, and I can't sleep. The drip in our bathroom shower is barely audible, but I know it's there. So it reverberates like a tormenting bass drum.

For the record, surrendering tonight's sleep has been my last resort. First, I cushioned the shower floor with a beach towel. While that worked for a while, eventually the woodpecker on autopilot came back to taunt me. So I attacked the showerhead with a crescent wrench. Again, solitude ensued, but only for a spell. The metronome from hell started ticking again. So I tried to become one with nature. You know, go with the flow. In my imagination every drip was a sheep clicking its hoof on the fence. A million sheep later they were still hurdling—with no sign of lamb chops in the immediate future. So I resigned myself to the inevitable and straggled out of bed.

Drip. Drip. Drip. Drip.

The drip seems an apt metaphor of life. After all, it's not the gushing current that sweeps you away; it's the unmerciful dribble of demands that eventually drowns you. In the equivalent of a flash flood, say, a loved one dies or you suffer a heart attack, well, then everybody understands. That's why we have insurance and bereavement fares and sick leave. But no one cuts you slack for a drip. Each drip is so quick there's no sympathy for the whiner who can't deal with it. Who wants to listen to someone snivel over a drip?

In many ways, I feel like a professional drip dodger—dancing around the demands of creditors whose bills are overdue.

"Not to worry," I promise a stressed editor, "I'll get you the manuscript by tonight. Sorry it's so late."

"Sweetie, after the sermon is written then Daddy will play with you."

"I meant to return your phone call but life has really been crazy."

"So I forgot to pick up diapers. Give me a break—maybe if I could stay at home all day then I'd have time to remember. I'd like to see you juggle everything I do at the office."

Drip. Drip. Drip. Drip.

I feel like a bookie in over my head, blubbering promises that nobody (including myself) believes anymore.

"Listen to me, Antonio. This Sunday I'll have some time and trust me, I'll get it done. You just have to believe in me."

I can relate to Philip Yancey's description of his pastor who "felt like an old hand-operated water pump, the kind still found at some campgrounds. Everyone who came to him for help would pump vigorously a few times, and each time he felt something drain out of him. Ultimately he reached a place of spiritual emptiness, with nothing more to give. He felt dry, desiccated."[1] I know that feeling.

Meanwhile . . .

Drip. Drip. Drip. Drip.

They say a drip can drive a person clinically insane. I wonder how close I've come to that edge. One Sunday morning comes to mind, when I disappeared down a deserted country road. I parked and cried. At first it was a whimper that eventually gave out to convulsing, jagged sobs. For hours I sat—paralyzed in a pile of teardrips.

I don't know why the emotional dam cracked; it just did. Maybe it was the board meeting when a church member demanded to see my Daytimer, asserting that "we're just not seeing any production out of our senior pastor." Maybe it was the ugly exchange of words with my wife when we acknowledged that our marriage was bordering bankruptcy. Maybe it was the constant chafe of guilt that I feel for preaching ill-prepared sermons or offering anemic prayers or dissing my kids in order to try and make a couple of petulant church members respect me. I'm not sure what prompted the breakdown, but I suspect it was just a little drip that broke the dam's back.

In that moment it occurred to me how shallow my life had become. I was skimming in every arena.

- I was skimming relationally—always promising to engage significantly in the life of my wife and daughters but never delivering. My intentions to do life deeply with more people were sincere but unrealized.

- I was skimming physically. Exercise, a healthy diet, adequate sleep—these were important values to me, but not essential to short-term survival. Thus they were activities I preached about but sporadically did.

- I was skimming professionally. While my churches always produced a veneer of success, I had the uneasy feeling that the house of cards might topple at any passing breeze.

- I was skimming emotionally. Because my life was chock full of eternal opportunities, I couldn't summon the courage to say "No." Ministry became a chore. I saw people as interruptions and recreation as a waste of time.

- Most of all, I was skimming spiritually. God was a distant notion that seemed so absent in the milieu of meaninglessness that marked my life.

A profound fatigue cast a shadow of hopelessness over my life. The relational, physical, professional, emotional, and spiritual reservoirs were dripping dry.

Drip. Drip. Drip. Drip.

The shallow puddle that sits in the shower paints a portrait of my soul. It's hard to anchor deeply in a puddle. Yet I yearn to go deeper, drinking ravenously from the wellsprings of Life and resting quietly in an artesian well of God's presence.

I have, in fact, begun that journey. It has taken me through the offices of Christian counselors, the mountains of Colorado for a sabbatical, the works of Henri Nouwen, Eugene Peterson, Philip Yancey, John Ortberg, and other gifted communicators, and to Scripture for life-breathing words of renewal.

In this quest to address the annoying drip of the soul, I have discovered that I am not alone. In numerous conversations friends have related similar feelings of fatigue. In a recent survey of my congregation the most pressing topic of interest was "soul fatigue." This capped my belief that we all aspire to take up the invitation of Jesus when he said, " 'Come to me, all you who are weary and burdened, and I will give you rest. Take my yoke upon you and learn from me, for I am gentle and humble in heart, and you will find rest for your souls' " (Matthew 11:28, 29).

Rest for your soul—sounds inviting, doesn't it? This book documents my pilgrimage through Scripture to find that rest and squelch the drip. If you, too, tire of the exasperating drip and seek a well-ordered soul, then this collection of stories and scriptures should serve you well. It's a how-to book on soul repair.

It is my story.

It is every seeker's story.

So dive in. As you do, I'll go call a plumber. I need some rest!

---

1. Philip Yancey, *Reaching for the Invisible God* (Grand Rapids: Zondervan, 2000), 73.

CHAPTER 1

Takin' Care of Busyness[1]

Every Wednesday, my wife goes to school as she aims at a Master's degree in education. While she listens to some esteemed university professor with lots of initials after his name, I am tutored by the wisest of all teachers—my three-year-old daughter, Lindsey.

Last week she gave a particularly brilliant lecture. I had planned a packed agenda for the day. The way I had it drawn up in my PalmPilot, we'd play Go Fish, hit the swing set, catch a bite for supper, and then cap it off with an hour at the pool. Much to my dismay, however, Lindsey couldn't get past our Go Fish game.

"Go, honey! It's your turn," I prompted.

"Wait!" she said, allowing herself to get distracted with an impromptu ballerina dance in the middle of the game. "Dee-da-dee-da-dee-dee-dum."

"Lindsey!" My veins were bulging, transforming my neck into a road map. "You asked me for a yak. I don't have it, so you have to go fish. Now go fish."

"Wait, Daddy! I'm doing a dance. Dee-da-dee-da-dee—"

"Lindsey! Sit down here and go fish. Hurry!"

That's when my miniature professor asked me a very profound

question. The question still hounds me. She asked, "Why, Daddy?"

I flunked her quiz. The question was so simple, yet it stumped me. I tried to answer but found myself asking the same question. Why did I insist on hurrying? Was it really that important to get through the game so we could go play on the swing set, scarf down supper, and then race to the pool? Was swinging or swimming any more worthwhile than spontaneously dancing? What's so holy about hurry anyway?

John O'Neil observes:

> Many people look at an overfull schedule as a badge of importance or popularity. For them, a heavily annotated calendar says, *Look at how important I am! How in demand! How many people and events depend on me!* An inflated ego is speaking. Self-inflation turns a busy life into a frantic one, testing our stamina, creating a lopsided set of priorities and values. Private time becomes a commodity so precious that we "save" it like something bankable. A man I know boasts that he needs fewer bathroom breaks during long meetings than any of his associates. Meyer Friedman, co-author of *Type A Behavior and Your Heart*, tells of a patient who made his meals in a blender so that he could save the time it takes to chew. An industrialist I know scheduled a fifteen-minute visit to his son's birthday.[2]

I can relate. One of my toughest struggles is taking care of busyness. I jitter like a humming bird on speed. I rush and race and run to do more. That's just the mad world that we live in, right? As Richard Swenson observes: "We send packages by Federal Express, use a long distance company called Sprint, manage our finances on Quicken, schedule our appointments on a Dayrunner, diet with Slim-Fast and swim in trunks made by Speedo."[3] Consequently, we live in a world of weary folk.

Mind you, it's not the kind of weary that can be cured by a good night's sleep. Nor is it the kind of weary that comes from strenuous exercise. Rather, it is a weariness of the soul. It is a fatigue of the spirit that prevents us from reaching our full spiritual potential. In our hurry we fail to love and trust God fully. We miss out on the joy of the kingdom—but not because we defy God. We are simply too fatigued, hurried, and preoccupied to follow Him. If Satan cannot make us curse God, he is content to make our lives so busy and unfocused that we skim in our devotion to the Lord.

Soul fatigue creates people who are always running, always behind, wishy-washy, superficial, disconnected from God, and too tired to care. We live in a world that pushes people into this way of life that does not make sense.

This was never God's design for His kids. There is a better way to do life. According to the prophet Isaiah, there is a source of healing to all who feel faint and spent.

The source of healing for soul fatigue

> Have you not known? Have you not heard? The LORD is the everlasting God, the Creator of the ends of the earth. He does not faint or grow weary; his understanding is unsearchable. He gives power to the faint, and strengthens the powerless (*Isaiah 40:28, 29, NRSV*).

Some years ago I registered with my friend Roger for a mini-triathlon. While the biking and jogging seemed doable, the swimming segment felt like an attempt to cross the Grand Canyon on a pogo stick. "It's only a quarter of a mile," Roger explained. "You couldn't drown if you tried."

"But, Roger, people drown in the bathtub."

"Sure, but that's different. They aren't competing."

"Huh?"

"Trust me, it's different."

"OK. It's different."

Next thing I knew we were diving into the frigid waters of Moses Lake. To survive among a thousand other swimmers I practiced my version of hydro Tae-Bo. After what seemed like the melting of an ice age, I finally carved a wake around the final buoy and thrashed toward shore. Collapsing on the sand, I looked up at Roger peering over me. I seemed to be hallucinating because his hair was dry. "Did you swim?" I asked. "Or was I so slow that you had time to go home and blow-dry your hair?"

"I went swimming," he smirked. "I walked right next to you the whole way. The water was never more than about four feet deep."

"Why didn't you tell me?"

"I wanted to, but it was too comical to watch you almost drown."

"You mean I almost drowned in water no deeper than my chest?"

"If it makes you feel any better, the water was deeper than your bathtub."

How often do we thrash and kick and panic, clamoring to survive, when the Source of Peace walks right beside us? *The LORD . . . gives power to the faint, and strengthens the powerless.*"

Soul fatigue was never God's plan for your life. He is the Source of healing for every person who feels weary and worn. This is good news, for who is better qualified for this role? After all, Jesus never felt worried or frantic. Remember the story in Mark 4, when Jesus and His friends were caught in a squall? The disciples panicked—but not Jesus. He simply commanded the storm, "Pipe down." Jesus felt all my human emotions—sorrow, joy, pain, anger, hope—except for one. He never worried. God is never in a hurry. He never panics.

It's good to remember that we have a God who is the Source of healing for all soul fatigue. This can breathe hope into every human spirit because we all wrestle with soul fatigue. Notice Isaiah's description of the universal scope of this condition.

The scope of soul fatigue

"Even youths will faint and be weary, and the young will fall exhausted" (Isaiah 40:30, NRSV).

Isaiah suggests that everyone is vulnerable to this condition of the spirit. Even youth feel the creeping menace of soul fatigue. Ever since the dawn of sin, humankind has felt this hunger of the heart. Ironically, in our age of plenty we are hungrier than ever when it comes to issues of the soul.

David Green, editor-at-large of *U.S. News & World Report,* writes:

> Men and women today are haunted by a sense that in the midst of plenty, our lives seem barren. We are hungry for a greater nourishment of the soul. In the England of today, a businessman turned philosopher, Charles Handy, has won a widespread following with his writing. Capitalism, he argues, delivers the means but not the point of life. Now that we are satisfying our outer needs, we must pay more attention to those within—for beauty, spiritual growth, and human connection. "In Africa," Handy writes, "they say there are two hungers . . . The lesser hunger is for the things that sustain life, the goods and services, and the money to pay for them, which we all need. The greater hunger is for an answer to the question 'why?' for some understanding of what life is for."

> In AD 1000, people could never truly satisfy their lesser hunger, but history suggests they were pretty good at fulfilling their greater one. Their lives were richer for it, and so were those that followed. A millennium later, our situation seems just the reverse. Is this really where we want to be? Or can we learn something from those poor folks, after all?[4]

The solution for soul fatigue

So what is the solution for soul fatigue? In a word, Isaiah claims the solution is to wait.

"Those who wait for the LORD shall renew their strength, they shall mount up with wings like eagles, they shall run and not be weary, they shall walk and not faint" (Isaiah 40:31, NRSV).

Those who *wait* for the Lord shall be renewed. But waiting does not come naturally to most of us. I hate to wait. I don't like it when my telephone conversation is interrupted with "Oops, I got another call.

Can you wait a second?" I don't like waiting at the airport. I don't like being at a stoplight sitting behind some accelerator-challenged driver when the light turns green. Waiting is not my spiritual gift.

Yet much of life is about waiting.

There's the waiting of the single person to see if God might have a partner in mind for him or her.

There's the waiting of a childless couple that yearns to start a family, but their prayer goes unanswered.

There's the waiting of somebody who longs to have work that seems to matter, but it doesn't happen.

There's the waiting of a deeply depressed person who hopes that he or she will wake up one morning with a desire to live, but that morning never seems to come.

There's the waiting of a spouse who is trapped in an abusive marriage that feels so hopeless.

There's the waiting of an elderly senior citizen in a nursing home for the mercy of death.

Listen to Lewis Smedes, from his book *Standing on the Promises*: "Waiting is our destiny as creatures who cannot by themselves bring about what they hope for. We wait in the darkness for a flame we cannot light, we wait in fear for a happy ending we cannot write. We wait for a not yet that feels like a not ever. Waiting is the hardest work of hope."[5]

In a word, it is God's solution for soul fatigue. Rather than rushing and hurrying and manipulating the circumstances of life, we are instructed to wait. Even though it is the hardest work of hope.

In Henri Nouwen's book *Sabbatical Journeys*, he writes about some friends of his who were trapeze artists. These circus performers called themselves the Flying Rodleighs. They told Nouwen of the special relationship between the flyer and the catcher on the trapeze. The flyer is the one who lets go, and the catcher is the one who catches. As you might imagine, that's a real important relationship—especially to the flyer. When the flyer is swinging high above the crowd on the trapeze, the moment comes when he must let go. As he arches in the air his job is to remain as still as possible and wait for the strong hands of the catcher to pluck him from the air. This trapeze artist told Nouwen, "The flyer must never try to catch the catcher. He must wait in absolute trust."[6] The catcher will catch him, but he must wait.

Perhaps you know that vulnerable feeling of waiting. You have let go of what it is that God has asked you to let go of, but you can't feel His hand catching you right now and you want to start flailing around. Will you just wait in absolute trust?

Wait on the Lord. For those who wait on the Lord *"shall renew their strength, they shall mount up with wings like eagles, they shall run and not be weary, they shall walk and not faint."*

Sometimes, Isaiah says, when you wait on the Lord you will soar with wings like eagles. What a magnificent picture! An eagle's wings are capable of catching rising currents of warm air, thermal winds that catapult the bird to speeds of eighty miles an hour. Without moving a feather, in breathtaking majesty, an eagle can soar to great heights.

For all who wait upon the Lord there will be seasons of soaring, times when you catch a gust of the Spirit. Jesus said, *"The wind blows wherever it pleases. . . . So it is with everyone born of the Spirit"* (John 3:8). Perhaps you are in an era of spiritual soaring right now. You find yourself borne up by God's power. God is shaping your life in extravagant and generous ways. He is granting you power to rise above temptation, flooding you with strength and wisdom beyond your ability. You're just soaring right now. If that's your condition, be very grateful. Do all you can do to stay in the stream of the Spirit's power. Never assume that you're soaring on your own strength.

Maybe you are not soaring. Instead you are running. Your spiritual journey is not effortless, but you are running the race. You're on course. You feel frustration, but you also feel God's pleasure in your obedience. If that's you, then keep running—faithfully following, serving, submitting, and giving. In God's own words, you *"shall run and not be weary."*

But there is a third line. Perhaps it is all you can do to *"walk and not faint."* Maybe your prayer goes something like this: "God, I don't feel very strong right now. I feel disconnected from You. I am wounded and weary. My soul is fatigued. But God, I will not let go. I will hang on to You, and I will just keep walking."

Wherever you find yourself these days, Jesus understands. He knows all about it. He knows about soaring. Think, for example, of the time He spoke the word and the tomb of His friend Lazarus filled with light. Or do you remember when the seventy-two disciples returned with glowing stories of the demons they trampled in God's name? How about the time Jesus stood on the Mount of Transfiguration? I think Jesus soared on those days.

But Jesus didn't always soar. He often encountered nasty obstacles in His mission on earth. His followers, for the most part, were disciple-challenged. When He faced resistance from the church leaders, Jesus just stayed the course. When Satan tempted Him in the wilderness, Jesus kept running.

But then the time came to climb a cross at Calvary. Jesus wasn't soaring on that day. When the cross was heaved on His bleeding back, He didn't scamper up The Way of the Skull. Although He was a young man, He stumbled and fell on that day. But He kept walking.

Sometimes walking is all you can do, but that's enough. In the hour when soul fatigue is most intense, it is enough to say, "God, I won't quit. Right now my life makes no sense, but I'll wait on You."

Do you ever feel entangled in a life of hurry that makes no sense? Are you consumed in busyness? Is your heart stressed? Your soul fatigued?

Then wait. Wait upon the Lord.

---

1. I am indebted for the inspiration of this chapter to two of John Ortberg's sermons: "Overcoming Soul Fatigue" (M9832), and "Waiting on God" (C9850) (South Barrington, Ill.: Seeds Tape Ministry, a ministry of Willow Creek Community Church, 1998).

2. John R. O'Neil, *The Paradox of Success* (New York: Putnam, 1993), 109.

3. As quoted by John Ortberg in the sermon, "Overcoming Soul Fatigue," preached on August 8, 1998, at Willow Creek Community Church, South Barrington, Illinois.

4. *U.S. News & World Report*, August 16-23, 1999, x.

5. Lewis Smedes, *Standing on the Promises* (Nashville: Thomas Nelson, 1998), 41, 42.

6. Henri J. M. Nouwen, *Sabbatical Journeys* (New York: The Crossroad Publishing Company, 1998), viii.

CHAPTER 2

My Life Is So Full... Why Do I Feel So Empty?

I tried not to gawk as I sat in a plush leather chair surrounded by brass and mahogany. The view from his office window smelled of heaven. Certificates and awards cluttered every shelf. It was a portrait of perfection—except for one thing. The man garnering all these ornaments of success was groveling in the corner like Jimmy Swaggert, confessing his sin.

"Pastor," he sobbed, "I can't do it any longer. My handicap at the country club is lower than it's ever been. I made in the seven digits last year alone. I own my own Lear jet. My kids are getting straight A's. And last night I almost swallowed a bucket of sleeping pills. I got everything I've always wanted, but I've never felt so lonely. My life is so full . . . why do I feel so #@*^# empty?"

I've been haunted by his question ever since. I've asked it a few times myself. Never have we been so pampered in luxury. These days we enjoy cushy cars and exorbitantly priced vacations. We can connect to the other side of the world in a heartbeat. We scan a hundred TV channels searching for the perfect entertainment. We can gorge at every meal. We are dizzy in delicacies. Never have our lives been so full.

And never have we been so drunk in depression.

According to the National Mental Health Association, half of Americans polled said they or their family members have suffered from depression, 46 percent considered it a health problem, and 43 percent saw it as a "sign of personal or emotional weakness." Of those polled, only 20 percent suggested that one might find relief from depression through God or the ministries of a church.[1]

Today, there is a famine of the spirit, yet few people look toward God for answers. In many ways, our condition reflects the heart cry of God's people in ancient times. Consider their story:

"In the second year of King Darius, on the first day of the sixth month, the word of the LORD came through the prophet Haggai to Zerubbabel son of Shealtiel, governor of Judah, and to Joshua son of Jehozadak, the high priest" (Haggai 1:1).

Notice how the book begins with a date. This is not a typical heading; rather, the date is significant because it highlights the fact that this is the first time God has directly communicated with His people since they were taken captive by the Babylonians. At the time of this writing, the Medes and Persians ruled the world.

The date also tips us off that it was a time of celebration. *"The first day of the sixth month"* was harvest time in Israel. Figs and pomegranates punctuated a season of surplus. That's when God spoke. Haggai relays a message to Zerubbabel, the political leader of Israel, and to Joshua, the spiritual leader of Israel.

"This is what the LORD Almighty says: 'These people say, "The time has not yet come for the Lord's house to be built" ' " (Haggai 1:2). The temple had been destroyed; twenty years prior to this pronouncement, the decree was given to rebuild the temple. But there was political opposition. The ruler, Cambyces, hated foreign cults—especially the Jews. Furthermore, there was opposition from some of the Jews! Whenever God's people rally to do something great to advance the kingdom, opposition emerges. No doubt, sometimes the loudest critics come from within the church. So God responds.

Then the word of the LORD came through the prophet Haggai:

"Is it a time for you yourselves to be living in your paneled houses, while this house remains a ruin?" Now this is what the LORD Almighty says: "Give careful thought to your ways. You have planted much, but have harvested little. You eat, but never have enough. You drink, but never have your fill. You put on clothes, but are not warm. You earn wages, only to put them in a purse with holes in it." This is what the LORD Almighty says: "Give careful thought to your ways" (Haggai 1:3-7).

Haggai sandwiches a profound observation between the command to *"give careful thought to your ways."* Here, God describes the way most people live. People were working harder, eating more, drinking more, earning more, and yet they were hungry, thirsty, and poor.

Symptoms of soul fatigue

Haggai observed how people were working harder and harder but their crops were yielding less and less. They were busier than ever and yet their dividends were dwindling.

Can you relate? Do you suffer from the same symptoms of soul fatigue? To diagnose, ask yourself a few questions: Am I usually rushed? Do I often complain that there are not enough hours in the day? Do I steam over the woman clogging up the express line at the grocery store with three too many items in her cart?

Can you identify with the Israelites who had all of their needs for food and water and clothing taken care of and yet they were not satisfied? Something was wrong, and that *something* had to do with the soul. Their discontentment could not be remedied by more stuff.

Even today, the notion that "stuff equals happiness" derails many. Let's face it, some of the smartest people in our world seek to sabotage your soul and convince you of two things: (1) you are unhappy; (2) happiness is only one purchase away.

Watch TV, study billboards, flip through a magazine, and a thousand products scream: "Try, buy, apply, taste, use, drive, sign, sip, smoke, wear, put me in your hair." You will be happy when you have a faster car and slower vacations, when you sport thinner thighs and bigger breasts, when you get a more tanned face and whiter teeth.

Dave Barry writes: "They have convinced us we need to spend money to alter every part of our body except our eyelid muscles, and its just a matter of time before someone comes up with a machine and an infomercial to sell that one."[2]

The most powerful treadmill of all is labeled "desire." Because no matter how fast you run on that treadmill, you never arrive at satisfaction.

So ask yourself: Do I have an insatiable appetite for more stuff? Or can I control my wants? As author Daria MonDesire writes:

> We all could benefit from fewer beepers going off, cell phones jangling, answering machines flashing, phones ringing and email waiting. Maybe if we defined our needs and tried to determine where our true values lie, mass advertisers wouldn't hold a death grip on our wants. The widening gyre of endless consumerism has us turning and turning. Unless we stop, we'll know nothing else.[3]

The heart cry of our society echoes that of the Israelites in Haggai's day: If my life is so full, why do I feel so empty? My life is so packed with busyness and choices and stuff and noise, how *could* I feel empty?

God's prescription for soul fatigue

In the verses that follow, God answers. Check out His prescription.

> "Go up into the mountains and bring down timber and build the house, so that I may take pleasure in it and be honored," says the LORD. "You expected much, but see, it turned out to be little. What you brought home, I blew away. Why?" declares the LORD Almighty. "Because of my house, which remains a ruin, while each of you is busy with his own house. Therefore, because of you the heavens have withheld their dew and the earth its crops. I called for

*a drought on the fields and the mountains, on the grain, the new
wine, the oil and whatever the ground produces, on men and cattle,
and on the labor of your hands"* (Haggai 1:8-11).

My life is so full, why do I feel so empty? God says it's because my
priorities are skewed. God tells His people: "Start building my house.
Start investing your money and energies in elements of the eternal. Stop
pursuing the trivial and start leveraging your resources into things that
matter."

Soul fatigue is cured only to the extent that we orient our affections
around the values of God's kingdom. We will never find relief from our
weariness until we go into the mountains and bring down timber—
that is, until we act and put the needs of God's kingdom above our own
carnal desires. God explains the spiritual void by saying, "My house lies
in ruins while you live in luxury. Therefore, I cannot bless you until I
have full dominion in your life."

The reality is that we will never find relief from our weariness until
we find refuge in our God. It's a truth captured in the following parable
passed down in many Jewish families.

Once upon a time, on an island kingdom, there lived a feeble man.
His eyes sparkled with wisdom gleaned through the years. Though ragged
in appearance, he showed tenderness in his nature. One day as he limped
through the forest, a gang of robbers attacked him. They swiped his
money and left him to die. The old man teetered between life and death
for some time until three soldiers happened by. They propped the old
man to his feet, attended to his wounds, and escorted him home.

A few days later, the soldiers called on the old man to see how he
was faring. The old man flashed a toothless grin and said, "I'm nearly
recovered! I owe my life to you boys. In return, I will grant you whatever you wish. But be very cautious, however, for you only get one
wish."

The soldiers snickered at the old man's seeming senility. After all,
who could grant another's wish? But they had nothing to lose, so they
humored him. The first soldier, who was rather poor, said, "Old man, I

have thought carefully, and I want wealth—lots of wealth." No sooner had he expressed the desire of his heart than a trunk of treasure appeared beside him. The other soldiers stared, dumbfounded at their colleague's fortune. The soldier thanked the old man sincerely and lugged his chest of gold out the door. As he left, the old man closed his eyes and felt sad. For he could see how the soldier would live comfortably with his wealth. He would entertain an army of buddies with the world's best food and wine. But the old man could also see that the soldier's riches would run out and the friends would disappear. He would be poor again.

Now the second soldier, who was particularly ugly, approached the old man and said, "I have thought carefully too, and my wish is to be handsome." Instantly, the soldier's face was transformed into a strikingly handsome appearance! He thanked the old man sincerely and danced out the door. As he left, the old man closed his eyes and felt sad. For he could see how the soldier would live happily with his good looks. He would boast of many friends—especially lady friends. But the old man could also see that as the soldier grew older, he would lose his good looks . . . and his friends. He would be ugly again.

Now the third soldier was stumped. For he was both poor and ugly. So he expressed his wish, thanked the old man sincerely and went home. As he left, the old man closed his eyes and smiled. For he could see that this soldier would remain poor and ugly all his life. Be he would live in peace, his soul would be fully satisfied. For the soldier's wish was simple— to seek first the kingdom of God. And to everyone's amazement, he was happy with whatever he had and however he looked. He really did live happily ever after.

---

1. *National and International Religion Report,* Jan. 1, 1992.

2. As quoted by John Ortberg in the sermon, "Overcoming Soul Fatigue" (M9832).

3. Daria MonDesire, "How Hard Should We Strive for Simple Life?" *USA TODAY,* 9 June 2000, A19.

CHAPTER 3

Against All Odds

Las Vegas odds-makers would tell you that Lee Capps should be dead. He's the man who was cruising in a small plane when his pilot friend suffered a massive heart attack and died. Although Lee had never flown before, he instinctively grabbed the microphone and cried for help. An air traffic controller responded, "Now just relax. I understand that you are having a problem here. Good news for you, I'm also a flight instructor. Would you be interested in a lesson?"

Being otherwise unoccupied, Lee Capps said, "Tell me anything and everything you know." The air traffic controller talked him through some basic maneuvers then blurted the inevitable. "OK, Lee, you're going to have to land. It's your only hope."

Lee Capps aligned the aircraft and headed toward the landing strip. The approach simulated the flight of a drunk duck. The landing looked more like the falling of a shot duck. But Lee Capps miraculously walked away with only minor injuries.

Following the touchdown, a reporter asked the air traffic controller whether he thought an untrained person like Lee Capps really had any shot at walking away. "Well," the answer came, "I knew it was a long shot but Lee Capps defied the odds."[1]

What are the chances?

Now in order to defy the odds, someone must first define the odds. So there are folk who do that for a living. For example, mathematicians in the know can tell you that your car is 38 times more likely to be stolen if it's a Corvette than if it's a Ford Escort wagon. (If you drive a Ford Pinto wagon, you can leave your keys in the ignition. It is mathematically impossible for it to be swiped!) The chances of being killed by a donkey are greater than dying in a plane crash. The odds of getting struck twice by lightning are greater than the odds of winning the state lottery.

Now usually the professionals who define the odds are very accurate, but not always. Someone will win the lottery. A neophyte pilot may land the plane. A Ford Pinto may be stolen—OK, maybe that's a stretch. But the point is, sometimes people defy the odds. Odds-makers can be dead wrong.

This is good news if you are staring at some steep odds right now. Perhaps you are fighting a chronic illness. Or you have a son who is far from God. Or your daughter is bulimic. Or your spouse is facing surgery. Or your mom has Alzheimer's. Or maybe you can't conceive the child you desperately want. Or you are mired in loneliness. Or your marriage is an emotional wasteland. Or you are one bad financial decision away from the bankruptcy court. Whatever your story, the odds feel impossible.

Before you collapse on the canvas for the count, consider the words of Haggai 2. The odds did not look good for God's people back then either. So God challenged them to face the impossible odds with courage. In spite of the circumstances, God provided peace.

Facing the odds

"On the twenty-first day of the seventh month, the word of the Lord came through the prophet Haggai: 'Speak to Zerubbabel son of Shealtiel, governor of Judah, to Joshua son of Jehozadak, the high priest, and to the remnant of the people' " (Haggai 2:1, 2). The date mentioned is significant because it marked the conclusion of the Feast of Tabernacles. God

is saying, "OK, you've had your party; now it's time to get to work."

The message was addressed to two men. First, to Zerubbabel, whose name literally meant seed *("zeru")* of Babylon *("Babel")*. That is to say, he was born in Babylon. The second man mentioned was Joshua, son of Jehozadak. We are tipped off that Joshua also was born during the exile, because we know that Jehozadak was the high priest of Israel during the Babylonian captivity. In this passage God speaks to His people who have just returned from Babylon, where they have been captive for sixty years. Keep in mind that the temple had been demolished in 586 B.C.

Through Haggai, God starts with three questions: " ' *"Who of you is left who saw this house in its former glory? How does it look to you now? Does it not seem to you like nothing?"* ' " (Haggai 2:3).

Question: If the temple was in such disarray for so long, why didn't the Jews get on it and start rebuilding?

Answer: Because the Israelites were as human as you and me. They allowed their fears to paralyze their production. They looked at the decimated temple, considered the political and internal opposition, performed a cost/benefit analysis and concluded: The odds for success are too high. So God recounts the glory years. He asks them, "Remember how the temple used to be?" Then God says, "It's time to face the overwhelming odds and recapture the faded glory."

Playing the odds: "Be strong"

That same whisper of hope can breathe courage for you today. You too can play the odds and win. How? God gives three suggestions to Israel.

First, He commands: " ' *"But now be strong, O Zerubbabel,"* declares the LORD. *"Be strong, O Joshua son of Jehozadak, the high priest. Be strong, all you people of the land,"* declares the Lord' " (Haggai 2:4). Back to back to back in rapid-fire succession, God trumpets the command, "Be strong."

As I think about people who have survived impossible odds, it occurs to me that a common denominator among them all is an inner strength. The first person who comes to mind is Cathy. I met Cathy at a seminar, where she was one of the presenters. As an interactive exercise, she listed a number of items and told us we had $100 to purchase whatever we wanted. The list included such things as wisdom ($30), a sense of humor ($45), peace ($35), joy ($40), and so on. After we made our lists and discussed them in a small group, Cathy resumed her lecture.

"By the way, Cathy," a student interrupted, "you never told us. How would you have invested your money?"

"Well, ah, I, um, . . ." The question caught her off-guard. Her eyes moistened. Her lip quivered. Then she shared her story. "Last year my son was playing Frisbee at the beach. It was one of those freak accidents that you never think could happen in your family. Well, he dove after the Frisbee in the water and landed on his neck. In that instant, he became paralyzed."

I glanced at her son sitting next to me. From his wheelchair, he smiled and nodded to encourage her. He, too, had leaking eyes.

"After his accident," Cathy continued, "I quit a job that I loved so that I could take care of my son. The only reason I did that was to keep hope alive. I could not watch him shrivel up in a sea of despair and hopelessness. So I vowed to journey through the tunnel with him in order to make certain he did not lose hope. In spite of the doctors' dismal projections, I have determined to be strong and hang on to hope. So I would spend my full wad of $100 on one thing—hope."

Cathy and her son remain a great inspiration to me. No matter what the odds, no matter how long the long shot, no matter how severe the loss, they are determined to be strong.

I think it's a wise investment indeed to throw everything we have into an arsenal of hope. Only then can we garner the courage to resist the onslaught of Satan's attacks. Lewis Smedes says, " 'Hope is as native to our spirits as thinking is to our brain. Keep hoping, you keep living. Stop hoping, you start dying.' "[2]

So don't slough off on hope. Be strong.

Playing the odds: "Work"

The second command is equally important. Don't stop reading too soon. Notice that God says, " ' *"Be strong . . . and work"* ' " (Haggai 2:4).

Too often we want to skip over the part about work. We want the road less traveled via the pathway of least resistance. Part of defying the odds, however, means doing the hard work of, well, work.

This was one of the lessons I learned in college. My freshman year was an education in itself. My buddy Steve and I learned a little about biology, a little about psychology, and a lot about work.

One of the most valuable lessons came on a Saturday night when we didn't have dates (which could refer to most every Saturday night). We went to Chattanooga to meet people. We met Rosita at Dunkin' Donuts. We chatted with Bob at Bob's Coffee & Donuts House. We spent a few minutes with Donna at The Donut Hole.

Much to our delight, we made an amazing discovery that evening—with a mixture of charm and coaxing, our new friends were willing to give us doughnuts. Free!

By 11:30 that evening we had a dozen lemon-filled, a half-dozen chocolate cremes, a dozen bear claws, and an arsenal of other sugar bombs to share with the guys in the dorm. (I don't even like doughnuts.)

The next Saturday night we didn't have dates. (You're beginning to understand why, aren't you?) Sitting in the dorm room, Steve said, "You know, I've been thinking. If it works for doughnuts, why wouldn't it work for pizza?"

Faster than we could say "cheese" we were racing toward the Pizza Hut on Third and Madison. We sauntered into the restaurant like Great Danes in a poodle convention.

"Smoking or non?" the cheery hostess greeted.

"We need to speak to the manager," I said.

The manager came to the counter. "How may I help you, gentlemen?"

"We were wondering, sir," Steve said tentatively, "if, um, you had some free pizzas sitting around. See, we're college kids with no money, no dates, and lots of time, so we thought you might like to help us out. Betsy, our old '79 Datsun, knows we're broke but she pulled into your parking lot anyway, so we thought we'd ask. What do you say?"

By now, the manager was smiling. "Sure, what kind do you want?"

"Everything vegetarian except pineapple," I replied. (I *do not* understand people who put pineapple on pizza. If God wanted fruit placed on pizza He would have created accordingly. The Bible is *very* clear on this.)

The evening flew by as we collected free pizzas around town!

The next Saturday night we had dates. (Scary, isn't it?) Intent on showering our dates with the finest amenities, we crashed a flower shop that week and went to work.

"We're a couple of poor freshmen," I started, "and have dates this weekend. We'd love to give our dates some corsages. Any chance you'd be willing to donate to a worthy cause?"

The pudgy lady behind the counter looked like a red "smiley face." "Sure!" she said with a gleam. "You boys remind me of my grandson. That's something like he would do. What kind of flowers should I put in the corsages?"

"I don't know," I said. "What kind are the most expensive?"

"Pink roses."

"Um, let's see, why don't we go with the pink roses this time."

The following Saturday night our dates looked fabulous sporting their five-rose corsages. They were the classiest ladies in the whole bowling alley!

Lounging around the room the following week, I wondered how far we could take our discovery. "If it works for doughnuts . . ." I mused.

"Yeah," Steve replied.

"And pizzas . . ."

"Yeah."

"And flowers."

"Yeah."

"Why wouldn't it work at the Honda dealer?"

The more we thought about it, the more we liked the idea. So we made our way to the dealership and requested a couple Honda XL250R motorcycles.

That experience taught us two valuable lessons. First, you don't get a free motorcycle unless you ask. Second, you don't get a free motorcycle even if you do ask (the Honda dealer looked as if we had asked him to bike to Mars). Because anything worthwhile in life, you have to pay for.

Count on it. Anything—career success, financial gain, athletic skills, relational authenticity, educational accomplishment, a deep faith—anything worthwhile in life you have to pay for.

Too many people settle for the doughnuts and pizzas and flowers in life, because they are unwilling to pay the price for what is truly valuable.

For the Israelites, part of playing the odds to increase their chances of recapturing the spiritual glory of the past required work. I suspect it's no different today. As Solomon put it, *"All hard work brings a profit, but mere talk leads only to poverty"* (Proverbs 14:23).

Playing the odds: "Remember God is with you"
The final counsel God offers comes as a reminder of His presence. In Haggai chapter 2 verse 5 God says, " ' *"This is what I covenanted with you when you came out of Egypt. And my Spirit remains among you. Do not fear."* ' "

Whatever the challenge you are facing, never forget that God is with you. Even when you shun Him, He pursues you. Never lose that deep confidence that no matter how impossible the odds may feel, God is with you. This is one of the great truths of spiritual life. This truth is captured in the adapted version of C. V. Garrett's story entitled "All the Way Back."

It was a hot sticky night in Miami. Brad could feel the heat rising from the sidewalk as he ambled down Biscayne Boulevard. Cars whizzed past, people walked by, sirens wailed. Brad did not feel a part of it. He wanted, in fact, to be apart. By himself. If only he could be alone—to pray aloud.

Sometimes silent prayer will not do. There are times when a man needs to hear the sound of his own voice reverberating to God. *If only there was a wayside chapel,* Brad thought, *or a church that was open.*

He walked on another two blocks. Then he stopped. He could hardly believe it, but there it was. A lovely glass door opened into a dimly lit chapel. Small wooden pews, a tiny altar, soft lighting. Perfect. Next to the door hung a sign: "Come in. You're welcome to sit, pray, meditate, or eat your lunch."

Brad noticed by the entrance a podium holding a guest book. A delightful idea. The book had columns for names, addresses, and comments. People from numerous states had autographed the book. In the comment column some had written evangelical statements: "Praise the Lord" or "Jesus saves" or "I have found Him here!" Many of them expressed appreciation for the very existence of such a place. Brad wrote a note expressing his good fortune in finding the wayside chapel.

Then the page blew back, and one statement caught his eye. In neat penmanship were written these poignant words: "Gail was here but left for good."

A pathetic statement. At best a flippant, feeble joke. At worst the sincere, desperate declaration of a soul. Brad thought it tragic either way, for it revealed a girl who was disillusioned. It was an expression of rejection of God.

The words stung Brad, so much so that when he seated himself in the rough-hewn pew he could think of nothing else. His own problems took a back seat to Gail's.

The prayers Brad longed to pray for himself were superseded by his concern for Gail and her soul. Kneeling in the dimly lit chapel, he lifted her to God in prayer. He prayed that God might reach down, reach out, reach in and save her.

With reluctance Brad left the little chapel. He had found a needed haven and in that place, a peace. He began his walk toward home.

He was only a few blocks from the chapel when an inspiration struck him. He turned around and began running. He ran all the way back.

Gail would hardly be there tonight. She had, after all, written that she would never return. Still she might come back sometime. The Spirit of the Lord could, in answer to Brad's own prayer, call her back for an unscheduled visit. And if so, she must know that someone cared, that God indeed cared.

Breathless, Brad opened the glass door and stepped inside the chapel. It was still empty. He turned to the visitor's book and picked up the pen. In the column beside the words "Gail was here but left for good" he wrote, "God was here and left for Gail."

Whatever season of struggle you find yourself in, remember that God is with you. He pursues you in your darkness. If you will resolve to be strong, work, and relax in the presence of God, chances are you will defy the odds. Such was the case for the Israelites in Haggai's day. Look at their triumph in the next paragraph.

Beating the odds

> *"This is what the LORD Almighty says: 'In a little while I will once more shake the heavens and the earth, the sea and the dry land. I will shake all nations, and the desired of all nations will come, and I will fill this house with glory,' says the LORD Almighty"* (Haggai 2:6, 7).

God promised His people that He would enter into the equation and tip the odds in their favor. His promise that the temple would be rebuilt smacked of impossible because the pitiful Jewish remnant was very poor. How would they ever be able to build and decorate a temple that would be worthy of the Lord?

Speaking to this issue, the Lord continues: " ' *"The silver is mine and the gold is mine"* ' " (verse 8). The book of Ezra tells us how God solved this problem. The locals objected to the Jews' rebuilding program and tried to stop it (see Ezra 5:1-17). But a search of empire records unveiled the fact that Cyrus had actually commanded that the temple be rebuilt! As a result, King Darius not only authorized the reconstruction but insisted that the costs *be fully paid out of the royal treasury, from the revenues of Trans-Euphrates* (Ezra 6:8). In essence, the enemies of the Jews bore the expense of rebuilding their temple!

Next comes the most implausible of all promises: " ' *"The glory of this present house will be greater than the glory of the former house," says the LORD Almighty. "And in this place I will grant peace," declares the LORD Almighty'* " (Haggai 2:9). The odds of this happening were about the same as Howard Stern and Kathie Lee Gifford getting married. Every Israelite knew of the grandeur of Solomon's temple. No doubt it was discouraging to compare their building project to what Solomon had accomplished. Yet God announced that " ' *the glory of this present house will be greater than the glory of the former house"* ' " (verse 9).

In spite of the impossible odds, God's promise proved true! For in the person of Jesus, God Himself visited the temple of the exiles. He preached the good news of salvation and peace. Thus He fulfilled the promise " ' *"And in this place I will grant peace."* ' "

Ever find yourself longing for that kind of peace? When the odds are piled against you and you're getting pummeled, wouldn't it be nice to live with perfect serenity? The truth is, you can.

Evelyn Underhill observes, "It is God's will for us that we should possess an Interior Castle, against which the storms of life may beat without being able to disturb the serene quiet within; a spiritual life so firm and so serene that nothing can overthrow it." And the prophet Isaiah put it this way: *"You will keep in perfect peace him whose mind is steadfast, because he trusts in you"* (Isaiah 26:3).

You can defy all odds and discover this peace. How? It comes through the indwelling Prince of Peace. Your part is to be strong. Work. And remember that God is with you.

---

1. As quoted by Bill Hybels in the sermon, "Against All Odds" (M9615), preached Easter weekend, 1996, at Willow Creek Community Church, South Barrington, Illinois.

2. Lewis Smedes as quoted from the publisher at www.barnesandnoble.com.

CHAPTER 4

Got Worry?

Do you ever worry? I recall an interview some years ago in which Erma Bombeck boasted, "I'm good at worry. I worry about introducing people and going blank when I get to my mother. I worry about a snake coming up through the kitchen drain. I worry about the world ending at midnight and getting stuck with three hours on a twenty-four hour cold capsule. I worry about getting into the *Guiness World Book of Records* under Pregnancy: Oldest Recorded Birth. I worry what the dog thinks when he sees me coming out of the shower. I worry about scientists discovering someday that lettuce has been fattening all along."

If you can relate to being a good worrier, then you should consider the words of Jesus in Matthew 6:25-34. Let your soul absorb the passage in its entirety, then we'll unpack it verse by verse.

"Therefore I tell you, do not worry about your life, what you will eat or drink; or about your body, what you will wear. Is not life more important than food, and the body more important than clothes? Look at the birds of the air; they do not sow or reap or store away in barns, and yet your heavenly Father feeds them. Are you not much more valuable than they?

Who of you by worrying can add a single hour to his life?

"And why do you worry about clothes? See how the lilies of the field grow. They do not labor or spin. Yet I tell you that not even Solomon in all his splendor was dressed like one of these. If that is how God clothes the grass of the field, which is here today and tomorrow is thrown into the fire, will he not much more clothe you, O you of little faith? So do not worry, saying, 'What shall we eat?' or 'What shall we drink?' or 'What shall we wear?' For the pagans run after all these things, and your heavenly Father knows that you need them. But seek first his kingdom and his righteousness, and all these things will be given to you as well. Therefore do not worry about tomorrow, for tomorrow will worry about itself. Each day has enough trouble of its own."

A more modern translation puts it this way: "Don't worry. Be happy." That's all Jesus was trying to say. He said it, however, in a very logical and practical way.

First, consider the logic. Jesus builds a pyramid of reasoning that supports His thesis. Not only does He build up to His thesis, but He supports it coming down on the other side as well. Look at it closely.

In verse 25 Jesus says not to worry about what you eat, drink, or wear. Let's call that point A. Then point B (verse 26) is an illustration from nature in which Jesus points to the birds of the air and observes how they " *do not sow or reap or store away in barns.*' "That's because the heavenly Father cares for them. All of this is building to the thesis in verse 27, when Jesus asks the rhetorical question, " *'Who of you by worrying can add a single hour to his life?'* "

The bottom line is that worry is useless. No one will live longer for having worried so of what value is it? To further support this contention, Jesus completes the line of reasoning by echoing points A and B. Notice how verse 28 (point B prime) is another illustration from nature. Jesus points out how the lilies do not labor or spin, yet they still grow. Then in verse 31 (point A prime) He once again gives the command not to worry about what to eat or drink or wear.

Graphically, the pyramid of logic would look like this:

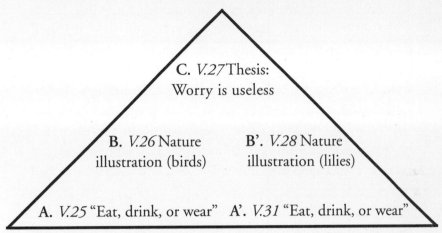

C. *V.27* Thesis:
Worry is useless

B. *V.26* Nature
illustration (birds)

B'. *V.28* Nature
illustration (lilies)

A. *V.25* "Eat, drink, or wear"   **A'.** *V.31* "Eat, drink, or wear"

Not only was Jesus logical in His treatise on worry, He was also very practical. For He did not just say "Don't worry." Everybody knows of the futility of worry. Who could argue that worry is productive? We all agree with the premise. Here's the question: How do we stop worrying? Notice Jesus' three suggestions on how to win the worry wars.

Trust God

The first step in winning over worry is to trust God. In verse 32 Jesus comments on how " *'the pagans run after all these things, and your heavenly Father knows that you need them.'* "The reasoning here makes sense. For pagans to worry about what to eat, drink, or wear is one thing. After all, they do not know God who can provide all these needs. But for Christians to worry over the essentials is ludicrous. After all, Christ-followers know of a heavenly Father whom they can trust to supply all human needs.

No doubt Jesus speaks truth about our culture when He observes that " *'pagans run after all these things.'* "A recent edition of *U.S. News and World Report* featured a cover story entitled "World-class Workaholics." The subtitle: "Are crazy hours and takeout dinners the elixir of America's success?"

Consider excerpts from the report:

Between 1977 and 1997, the average workweek (among salaried Americans working 20 hours or more) lengthened from 43 to 47 hours. Over the same years, according to James T. Bond, vice president of the Families and Work Institute, the number of workers putting in 50 or more hours a week jumped from 24 percent to 37 percent. Scarcely a decade ago, Americans viewed the work habits of the Japanese with half-horrified awe. Now, according to a recent report of the International Labor Organization, the United States has slipped past Japan to become the longest-working nation in the advanced industrial world.[1]

Why our obsession over work? According to the report, it is fueled by our worry over our basic needs—what we eat, drink, and wear. Case in point: Mary Fowler, who is 53, lives with her two grandchildren in Baltimore, and works as a school custodian. A year ago, an ambulance took her to the hospital after she passed out while cleaning up in a portable school annex. "It was hot," she recalls. Although she left the next morning with a clean bill of health, the tab came to $3,000. Fowler had no medical insurance. To pay for her hospitalization, she took a weekend job as a caterer. To free up the time, she cut down on her volunteering at a local church.

The article continues: "With the erosion of big-company pension plans and doubts about the long-term viability of Social Security, many Americans feel pressed to work harder in order to pump up their savings—even as they steel themselves to work until they are 70 or older."[2]

Consequently, our workaholic ways poison the quality of our lives. For example, consider the impact on the family. According to Ellen Galinsky's book *Ask the Children*, the biggest complaint of kids is that frazzled parents can't slow down. Unfortunately, many children of hardworking parents have never experienced anything else. That's because we act as if we have no other choice but to be obsessed by work. Our assumptions go unchallenged. Amy Saltzman observes:

In many ways it has always been easier to act as if there were no options; as if we didn't have a choice. Accepting the standard definition of work success frees us from experiencing any existential angst about what to do with our lives. "The idea of decreasing work is hair-raising for many people," says Benjamin Kline Hunnicutt, a professor of leisure studies at the University of Iowa and author of *Work Without End*, a study of America's growing work culture in the years following the Depression. "If we worked less we would suddenly be confronted with the problem of freedom and what to do with it. Work is an escape from freedom." But in allowing us to avoid the possibilities offered by freedom, the fast track shackles us to a set of standards and rules that prohibit us from leading truly successful, happy lives.[3]

Jesus offers us the freedom to live "truly successful, happy lives." The key to this life of joy is to trust Him fully.

Recently, I received a letter from a preacher's kid who knew firsthand the experience of living with parents who can't slow down. After offering high praise for my ministry, she concluded the letter with the following paragraph:

> I realize that part of why your ministry has been so spectacular is that you have put so much of your time and soul into it. This letter is only sent as a reminder that your children will be affected—both positively and negatively—by your actions today. I pray that God will continue to use you in such powerful ways, and that your family will have the privilege of having YOU—your attention, your time, your soul—as well.

I'm keeping that letter as a reminder of what Jesus taught when He said, "It makes sense for pagans to live frantic and frenzied lives that are out of control. But as My disciples you should enjoy peace and balance, for you know that your heavenly Father cares for the lilies and birds, and He will also care for you. Just trust."

Seek first God's kingdom

The second way to combat worry is to put first things first. Jesus said, " *'But seek first his kingdom and his righteousness, and all these things will be given to you as well'* " (verse 33). The ocean of worry we're drowning in begins to evaporate when we orient life around that one all-consuming passion—to seek first the kingdom of God.

Too often it is easy to get in a tizzy trying to dazzle others. No wonder we worry! The applause of people is fickle and fleeting. Furthermore, it is never fully satisfying. Yet how many of us structure our lives around this elusive fantasy of pleasing everyone?

I'm embarrassed to tell you how often I find myself seeking first the approval of others rather than living to please an audience of One. Too often, image management controls my behavior. I'm obsessed with working and living in such a way as to paint myself in the best possible light. I work hard to secure the applause of people. The irony is that the cheers are so shallow.

I was reminded of this on a recent trip to Hollywood, California. As a diversion to an endless docket of meetings, I slipped over to Burbank to catch a taping of the "Tonight Show" with Jay Leno. Following the show, NBC staffers were recruiting audience members for another show they were taping called "Later." With time to waste I shuffled in the crowd toward Studio B-1, where we waited. And waited. And waited. Some guy tried to entertain us with jokes. That wasn't working so he suggested that we practice the beginning of the show when the host would take the stage. He said, "I need someone to be our superstar." He looked right at me.

I quickly broke eye contact. No way would I volunteer.

I didn't need to. He pointed at me and said, "You sir, in the green Sterling Savings T-shirt, why don't you be our superstar?"

I said, "No, um, that's OK."

But he insisted, "Yes, you. Come down here."

I had no choice, so I joined him on the stage. "What's your name?" he asked.

"Karl Haffner."

"Where you from?"

"Walla Walla, Washington." Everybody in the audience busted up laughing.

"No really," he said, "where are you from?"

I repeated myself—much to the delight of people who had never heard of the "city so nice they named it twice."

Next he said, "What do you do for a living?"

"I'm a pastor." (Audience explodes in laughter.)

"No, really, what do you do for a living?"

"That's what I do."

"Really! And what denomination?"

I said, "Seventh-day Adventist." (Audience explodes in laughter.)

"No really, what denomination?"

After noting the details of my life, they sent me off stage into the makeup room. Suddenly the announcer bellowed, "And now, all the way from Walla Walla, Washington, the infamous Seventh-day Adventist pastor that you all know and love. That's right, tonight on 'Later' we have him here in our studio. Please welcome the one, the only, Kaaaaaaaaarl Haffner."

Serenaded by the wild accolades of the studio audience, I shuffled onto the stage. They were all cheering as though the President had just canceled all taxes. Every one was standing. The orchestra was blasting. People were throwing money at me—OK, so the story grows in my own mind. But they really were going crazy as if to say, "We love you and the mother who bore you."

As soon as the lights dimmed, however, silence swallowed the room. Everyone sat down.

In that moment it hit me—the applause of people really is that fickle and fleeting. Nevertheless, many of us direct our lives toward securing their applause.

I'm weary of that empty pursuit. How about you? I want to live for an audience of One. I want to hear God say, "Well done." I want to seek *first* His kingdom and then everything else will take care of itself.

Live one day at a time

The final step is to live one day at a time. Jesus concludes, " *'Therefore do not worry about tomorrow, for tomorrow will worry about itself. Each day has enough trouble of its own'* " (verse 34).

In her book *Celebrate Joy!* Velma Seawell Daniels talks about this familiar phrase. She tells of interviewing a man who had made a trip to Alaska to visit people who live above the Arctic Circle.

"Never ask an Eskimo how old he is," the man said. "If you do, he will say, 'I don't know and I don't care.' And he doesn't. One of them told me that, and I pressed him a bit further. When I asked him the second time, he said, 'Almost—that's all.' That still wasn't good enough for me, so I asked him 'Almost what?' and he said, 'Almost one day.' "

Mrs. Daniels asked him if he could figure out what the Eskimo meant. He answered that he did but only after talking to another man who had lived in the Arctic Circle for about twenty years. "He was a newspaperman who had written a book about the Eskimos and their customs and beliefs. He said the Eskimos believe that when they go to sleep at night they die—that they are dead to the world. Then, when they wake up in the morning, they have been resurrected and are living a new life. Therefore, no Eskimo is more than one day old. So, that is what the Eskimo meant when he said he was 'almost' a day old. The day wasn't over yet."

"Life above the Arctic Circle is harsh and cruel, and mere survival becomes a major accomplishment," he explained. "But, you never see an Eskimo who seems worried or anxious. They have learned to face one day at a time."[4]

Have you learned how to put worry and anxiety aside and live one day at a time?

Don't worry

Recently, I was stranded on my way to speak at a conference in Kansas City. After a three-hour mechanical delay in Denver, the announcement came that there were thirteen seats on another flight. More than 300 people swarmed to the new gate. While anxiously waiting, the woman next to me struck up a conversation.

"Where you going?" she asked.

"I need to get to Kansas City by tonight. I am the keynote speaker for a conference there."

"I'm going to Kansas City too. I work for United so I am hoping for the jumpseat, but it doesn't look good."

She carried the conversation while I worried. Abruptly, she stopped mid-sentence and said, "Sir, do you know there is absolutely nothing you can do in this situation? The FAA won't let you out there to fix the broken plane, and as for the limited seats on this one, either they will put you on or they won't. It has to do with your premiere status and the flight miles you have logged this year. There is nothing you can do to change what is going to happen. So if you don't mind, could you please relax? Your fidgeting is driving me crazy."

"Sorry," I squirmed. "I didn't even realize that I was worrying."

As it turned out, I did get on the flight. I arrived in time to present my talk. And I was reminded one more time that worry really is useless.

---

1. James Lardner, "World-class Workaholics," *U.S. News & World Report,* 20 December 1999, 42.

2. Lardner, "World-class Workaholics," 48.

3. Amy Saltzman, *Downshifting: Reinventing Success on a Slower Track* (New York: HarperCollins, 1992), 23.

4. As quoted in *Bible Illustrator,* Parsons Technology, index 3020, 3021.

CHAPTER 5

In the Cave, but Not Caving In[1]

The devil had a garage sale. Did you hear about it? His tools were on sale to anyone willing to pay the price. Pride, envy, lust, anger, and deceit were but a few of the classics on display.

In the corner was a wedge-shaped tool. Scrapes and scratches marked its handle. The iron head was worn and dull. The tattered canvass case disclosed a lifetime of use. In spite of its condition, however, the tool displayed a price tag higher than any other tool.

"Why in this hell," a curious shopper asked, "would that old tool be so blame expensive?"

"Ahhhhh," the devil smirked. "That's my most useful tool. I call it discouragement. With it, I can dig into a person's heart and live forever. With it, I can suck the joy and wonder right out of life."

Discouragement destroys. Discouragement fatigues the soul like nothing else. It taints our friendships, our feelings, and our future. Discouragement is like a cancer that gobbles up our vital optimism. And without vital optimism, we shrivel up and miss the whole adventure that God has in mind.

So how is your discouragement quotient these days? Do you ever find yourself caving in to the negative impulses that permeate our culture? Do you find yourself in a cave, surrounded by darkness? If so, you will be well served to consider a chapter out of the life of David. He too found himself in the cave, but he refused to crumble under the dome of discouragement.

David in the cave

David had a promising future. He was anointed by Samuel to be the next king. He defeated Goliath, and the army loved him. People wrote songs about him. Then a funny thing happened on his way to the palace.

One by one the blessings were stripped away. First, David lost his job. Because of Saul's pathological jealousy, David went from being the most successful officer in the army to a fugitive fleeing for his life. Next, David lost his wife and family. Because his wife, Michal, was also Saul's daughter, the marriage imploded. Then David fled to Ramah, where Samuel, his spiritual mentor, lived. There he would find refuge—or so he thought. Instead, no matter how far David ran, it wasn't far enough. Saul sent his soldiers to Ramah, and David had to make another escape. So David went to his best friend, Jonathan. At last he was with the one person that he could trust fully. Jonathan stood up to his own father, Saul, and risked his life for David. But Jonathan could not leave the court or raise a sword against his father. So David ran for his life once again.

How quickly the landscape of life can change. The Bible records that after this avalanche of loss, *"David left Gath and escaped to the cave of Adullam"* (1 Samuel 22:1). Remember that this is a man who is expecting the palace. He is waiting for the throne. He had wealth, power, beauty, fame, friends, security, and what he thought was a guaranteed future. And now all that's gone. No money, no home, no friends, no job, no advisors, and he's running for his life. He's expecting a palace, but he ends up in a cave with no explanation of why and no guarantee that it will ever be over. David is in the cave.

Perhaps you know the feeling. The cave is where you end up when all of your scaffolding gets stripped away. Maybe you've lost a job, or you're under financial pressure. Perhaps your dreams of a family have been shattered. Maybe you've lost a spouse to death or desertion or divorce. Maybe you've lost a mentor or a very good friend. Maybe your cave involves a physical condition. Maybe you made a bad decision and everything is crashing in. For whatever reason, you're in the cave.

It's in the cave when we often wonder, "Has God lost track of me? Has God forgotten His promises? Does God remember where I am? Does He even hear? Will I ever be anywhere but this cave? Will I die here?"

Take heart. Caves are where God does some of His best work. That's where he molds and shapes human lives like no other place. When all the crutches get kicked out from under you and you find that all you have left is God, you then discover that God is enough.

Such was David's discovery. Look at 1 Samuel 22:1, 2.

David left Gath and escaped to the cave of Adullam. When his brothers and his father's household heard about it, they went down to him there. All those who were in distress or in debt or discontented gathered around him, and he became their leader. About four hundred men were with him.

In spite of the horrendous darkness enveloping David, he had a small community for support. But notice the description of this ragtag group of guys— *"all those who were in distress or in debt or discontented."* Who wants to hang with friends like that?

From there it only got worse. Their families were taken captive by the Amalekites. Rebellion erupted from within the ranks. And the story culminates in 1 Samuel 30:4: *"So David and his men wept aloud until they had no strength left to weep."*

Have you been there? Have you ever wept until you had no more strength to weep? I have.

One Friday I received news that my older sister was diagnosed with cancer. The C-word felt like a death sentence. The following day in church I didn't mention it to anybody even though my thoughts were consumed by the news. After the service, a couple who had been very active in the formation of the church approached me and ripped into me with a litany of complaints. They griped about how unsupported they felt in the ministry they were involved with; they complained about the shallow nature of my sermons and the direction we were going as a church. They threatened to transfer their membership. On and on they snarled.

I couldn't dismiss myself from the sanctuary soon enough and retreat to the closet that served as my makeshift office. It was a dark and musty office, similar to a cave. I collapsed in the corner and wept for two hours. I felt like David.

> *So David and his men wept aloud until they had no strength left to weep. David's two wives had been captured—Ahinoam of Jezreel and Abigail, the widow of Nabal of Carmel. David was greatly distressed because the men were talking of stoning him; each one was bitter in spirit because of his sons and daughters. But David found strength in the LORD his God* (1 Samuel 30:4-6).

I hope you didn't skip over that final line. Check it out again. *"But David found strength in the LORD his God."* Ellen White writes: "In this hour of utmost extremity, David, instead of permitting his mind to dwell upon these circumstances, looked earnestly to God for help."[2]

The King James Version reads, *"But David encouraged himself in the LORD."* It's a wonderful thing to be encouraged by other people. It's great to read a book or listen to a tape or confide in a counselor who renews your spirit. But when you're in the cave with nobody to lean on and you learn how to be encouraged by God alone, you start growing real strong. This is a great secret of spiritual life.

Ruby Bridges tapped into this secret. You may remember this six-year-old dynamo from your history books. She's the girl in New Orleans who opted to attend school after a federal judge forced schools to open their doors to both Black and White kids. Consequently, most

White parents kept their children home. Some parents went so far as to threaten any Black students who attended school, so most of the Black students stayed home too—except for Ruby.

Every day, this girl would wake up, have breakfast, brush her teeth, kiss her mom and dad goodbye, and walk out the door to school. She didn't ride the bus, she didn't go with other kids, nor did she venture out alone. Ruby was flanked by four federal marshals. For in order to get to that empty school building she had to pass through a hostile crowd that would swarm the streets.

They'd yell, swear, and threaten her for going to school. Nevertheless, every morning at ten minutes to eight Ruby walked through the mob with her head up and her eyes glaring straight ahead. She walked into the empty school building to learn, and then she'd walk back home.

What is most amazing is not that she kept coming back, but the spirit with which she did it. A White schoolteacher described what she saw when Ruby walked into the school. She said:

> "I was standing in the classroom, looking out the window, and I saw Ruby coming down the street, with the federal marshals on both sides of her. The crowd was there, shouting, as usual. A woman spat at Ruby but missed; Ruby smiled at her. A man shook his fist at her; Ruby smiled at him. Then she walked up the stairs, and she stopped and turned and smiled one more time! You know what she told one of the marshals? She told him she prays for those people, the ones in that mob, every night before she goes to sleep!"[3]

Can you imagine? A six-year-old praying, "God bless the people who are so mad at me. God bless that woman who spit at me. God bless that man who shook his fist in my face. God help them."

Dr. Robert Coles, a Harvard psychiatrist, wondered what could create that kind of spirit in a six-year-old. So he interviewed Ruby, her family, and other people involved. In his book, *The Moral Life of Children,* he wrote that the best he could discern it, conventional psychiatric language and psychological concepts could not explain this girl or her courage. He writes:

> If I had to offer an explanation, though, I think it would start with the religious tradition of black people, which is often of far greater significance than white observers, and possibly a few black critics, have tended to allow.
>
> In home after home, I have seen Christ's teachings, Christ's life, connected to the lives of black children by their parents. . . . Such a religious tradition connects with the child's sense of what is important, what matters.[4]

When forced to explain why Ruby could live in a cave so dark without caving in, one of the brightest minds in the world retreats to an explanation that defies logic. His only answer: "It's Jesus."

When life got real difficult, Ruby tapped into a supernatural power that gave her the strength and courage to endure. How did she secure that kind of stamina in the storm? Like David, she found her strength in God. The good news is that you and I can plug into the same power source. How?

Resist the shortcut

First, we must resist the temptation to take a shortcut out of the cave. Whenever you're in the cave you will be vulnerable to any temptation that promises relief from the darkness. It is important, however, not to compromise long-term character for short-term comfort. Your cave is not a prison of punishment. Rather, it is a classroom where God can craft your character in ways that will never happen when life is coasting on cruise control. Thus, you must not yield to the tantalizing whispers of the temptress who promises a quick ride out.

David faced this temptation to short-circuit what God wanted to do in him through the cave. Consider his temptation:

> *After Saul returned from pursuing the Philistines, he was told, "David is in the Desert of En Gedi." So Saul took three thousand chosen men from all Israel and set out to look for David and his men near the Crags of the Wild Goats. He came to the sheep pens along the way; a cave was there, and Saul went in to relieve himself. David and his men were far back in the cave. The men said, "This is the day the LORD spoke of when he said to you, 'I will give your enemy into your hands for you to deal with as you wish' "* (1 Samuel 24:1-4).

This is David's ticket out of the cave! While the writer tells us more about Saul than we really care to know, he does graphically portray Saul's vulnerability. David's men immediately see the exit door out of the cave. They even suggest that God has provided the escape hatch. Their reasoning resonates with logic. "This must be what God wants," they contend. "God doesn't want you to be unhappy and miserable in this cave. God promised the throne to you, and now He's proving good on His promise. Seize it! Saul deserves judgment. This is a clear way out of the cave. It must be God's will."

David will not bite.

> *Then David crept up unnoticed and cut off a corner of Saul's robe. Afterward, David was conscience-stricken for having cut off a corner of his robe. He said to his men, "The LORD forbid that I should do such a thing to my master, the LORD's anointed, or lift my hand against him; for he is the anointed of the LORD." With these words David rebuked his men and did not allow them to attack Saul. And Saul left the cave and went his way* (1 Samuel 24:4b-7).

It must have been so tempting for David to think, *I could get out of the cave now.* It would have been a shortcut, however, and it could well have sunk David's legacy. It certainly would have sent a message to everybody in Israel that the way to become king is to kill the old one.

If you are in a cave right now, no doubt there is a shortcut seducing you. So will you submit to God's plan? Or are you going to take things into your own hands?

Maybe you feel lonely because you've been single a long time or your marriage is empty. There's another relationship that promises intimacy. It's tempting to think, *This is so available, and it would feel so good. I'm miserable and lonely in this cave. This must be God's will! After all, He wants me to be happy, right?*

Rubbish! It's a shortcut.

Maybe you face financial temptation. A little fudging here, some creative accounting there, and you can build a bridge to solvency. God must be paving the way, right?

Nonsense! It's a shortcut.

Perhaps you have an addiction that numbs the pain enough to allow you to cope. While you know that someday God wants you to overcome this pattern of sin, for now it's not a big deal. God understands, right?

Hogwash! It's a shortcut.

While the shortcut can provide relief in the moment, it will ultimately destroy your soul. So don't think that the easy way out is an easy way out. If you are serious about finding your strength in the Lord, first you must pass on the shortcut. Instead, you must rest in the shelter of God.

Rest in the shelter of God

While he was in the cave, David resigned himself fully to God. Psalm 142 is subtitled, "A maskil of David. When he was in the cave." This is a psalm of the cave. David writes:

> *When my spirit grows faint within me, it is you who know my way. In the path where I walk men have hidden a snare for me. Look to my right and see; no one is concerned for me. I have no refuge; no one cares for my life. I cry to you, O LORD; I say, "You are my refuge"* (Psalm 142:3-5).

Even in the darkest of caves, David could proclaim God as his ultimate refuge. Likewise, to keep from caving in to the pressure of the cave, you must rest in the shelter of God.

It is important to understand what this means and also what it does not mean. Resting in the shelter of God implies an abiding confidence that He will sustain you in the cave. It is the unshakable faith that God will not forsake you no matter how dark and desperate you feel. This does not mean, however, that you will be delivered from the cave on this earth.

Too often stories circulate in Christian circles, which imply that faith is the ticket to a pain-free existence. Well-meaning Christians suggest that if you just have enough faith (say, a mustard seed or so) then you wouldn't be in the cave. My reaction to this theology is *"BUNK!"* Nowhere in Scripture can you find the notion that Christians who possess enough faith can manipulate circumstances in life to circumvent the caves. Hardships bruise the faithful as much as the faithless. Stories that suggest otherwise don't square with the reality of life.

I think of the experience of my brother Paul and his wife Fae. After four miscarriages they were expecting again. The fears were ignited all over again that this pregnancy would result as every other one that left them choking in grief. I was reticent to say it to them once again, but I responded to the news of another pregnancy by promising, "I will pray and pray and pray for you."

"What good will that do?" Paul snapped. "We have prayed every time and it hasn't worked so far. Maybe this time we should not pray and see what happens. Or . . . maybe we'd have four kids now if we just had enough faith and prayed more."

Following that conversation I left home to attend a pastor's meeting. Seventy-five ministers from our conference huddled in the lodge at Sunset Lake Camp. We began in the customary fashion—sharing prayer concerns. One pastor shared a "prayer praise" of how he and his wife were walking one stormy night when she lost her wedding band.

When he started the story I knew immediately where it was heading. Sure enough, the tale unfolded as expected. "We looked and looked and looked for that wedding band with no luck. Then we prayed. We knelt in the pouring rain right there on the public street," the pastor paused for dramatic effect. "When we opened our eyes we both spotted the ring immediately!"

The punch line sparked an enthusiastic ovation. A chorus of "Hallelujah! Praise the Lord!" filled the room.

Now I don't mean to disparage my colleagues or the "miracle," but do you know how that testimony hit me? I started to shake with anger. My eyes moistened with rage. Dismissing myself from the lodge, I escaped to the woods where I could scream at God, "What in the name of heaven or hell are You doing? Why do You answer a frivolous prayer to find a ring and ignore the heart cry of barren parents? God, I'd buy her a stupid wedding band if You would just answer our prayer."

Such stories imply that being in the cave is our fault. Furthermore, it suggests that getting out of the cave is up to us as well. That is to say, if we just pray and manufacture enough faith, then we can find the ring or bear a child or overcome cancer or save the marriage. In my opinion, such reasoning constitutes a flawed understanding of faith.

Let me repeat. Faith is not a ticket to a pain-free life. Nor is it about doubt-free certainty. Sometimes faith means just hanging on. *Faith is sitting in the cave surrounded by darkness but trusting God anyway.*

My brother's spiritual journey landed on this understanding. Recently, he shared excerpts from his journal written during that dark chapter in the cave. "God" he wrote, "would it kill You to answer this prayer? Would heaven fall? Don't You think You could answer just this one thing? Why are You so silent? Why are You so distant? I feel like chucking it in. I'm not even going to keep trying. I don't even know if You're there. You are so silent."

Sometimes faith means that you wait in the cave, helpless to escape in your own power. You can only hang on.

My brother matured to this understanding. He grew to see that faith is not about getting what you want. Faith means tenaciously holding on to the hand of God. It's about refusing to take a shortcut and resting in the refuge of God.

So Fae got pregnant again. By this point, however, Paul came to an understanding that the birth of the child was beyond his control. It wasn't about mustering enough faith in order to preserve the child's life. He came to realize that faith is not a fertilizer to the womb, nor is it a way to control pain; rather, faith is trusting through the pain. So this is what he wrote in his journal:

> March 7, 1996
> Dear God,
> I thank You for the baby You are growing right now in Fae. I dedicate that baby to You. I don't know that the baby will grow up to be a religious leader by dedicating him to You; perhaps that doesn't matter as much as that he grows up with an irrational love for You.
> I thank You for the gift, yet I submit to You. If we don't keep this baby, then so be it. I still submit, and I still praise You. As I write these words there is a knife cutting through my heart at the thought. I don't want to lose this child. It aches through my body to even think that. But I know I must hang on to things—including my child—quite loosely. I almost feel like a sicko to even say this to You, God—please don't take the child if there is any way. I don't want to go through that again. But I covenant to hang in there with You. I feel like Abraham at the altar at Moriah. I don't want to let the child go. There seems no sense in it. But I will obey, and I will allow You to be God. In a weird sort of way, I thank You for being ruler of my life even through the hard and painful. Please God, hear my prayer and know my heart. Amen.

Sometimes faith is just hanging on to the hand of God as you sit in darkness. For Paul and Fae, their prayers were finally answered in the way of two healthy baby boys. But the story does not always end that way. A child is not always born. The wedding band is not always found. That's reality. So God wants to mature each of His children to the point of true trust—hanging on to Him, irrespective of the outcome.

Jesus in the cave

If you find yourself in a cave, please know that God understands all about caves. He has been there. Jesus suffered *like* us and He suffered *for* us. The Son of David also had everything stripped from Him. He lost His status as a teacher; His friends abandoned Him; His disciple betrayed Him; the cheering crowd mocked Him; and then He went to a cross and died. Soldiers put His body in a cave. They thought He was finished.

The enemy, however, forgot that God does some of His best work in caves. Caves are where God resurrects dead stuff. They put Jesus in a cave, but it was only for three days. They could not keep Him there. On Sunday morning, He exploded out of the darkness. Jesus was not imprisoned in His cave forever.

Nor will you be in your cave forever. Someday you too will explode out of the darkness. You will feel God's embrace, and you will be warmed by His close presence. It may not happen today or next week. It may not happen until Jesus comes again, but faith believes that someday it will happen. Someday . . .

Until that day, you resist the shortcut. Rest in the shelter of God. And remember that God does some of His best work in caves.

---

1. I am indebted for the inspiration of this chapter to a downloaded manuscript of John Ortberg's Sermon: "David: Developing A Heart for God; Hope for the Discouraged Heart" (C9943). http://www.willowcreek.org

2. Ellen G. White, *Patriarch and Prophets* (Nampa, Idaho: Pacific Press, 1958), 692.

3. Robert Coles, *The Moral Life of Children* (New York: Atlantic Monthly Press, 1986), 22, 23.

4. Coles, 34.

CHAPTER 6

Do You Really Want to Be Healed?

I collect bizarre questions. Check out a slice of my collection:

Why do they sterilize needles for lethal injections?

What was the best thing before sliced bread?

Why is it that the first piece of luggage coming out at the airport baggage claim doesn't belong to anyone?

Is there another word for synonym?

Why did kamikaze pilots wear crash helmets?

Why are there interstate highways in Hawaii?

If the cops arrest a mime, do they tell him he has the right to remain silent?

Why do you press harder on a remote control when you know the battery is dead?

So . . . what's the speed of dark?

Why do drive-through ATMs have Braille instructions?

If a cow laughs, does milk come through its nose?

I love bizarre questions. Perhaps that's why I am so intrigued with Jesus' question in the gospel of John. It's the most bizarre question in Scripture.

One day Jesus was moving through the streets of Jerusalem when

He happened upon a man who had been crippled for thirty-eight years. Because of His reputation as a healer, Jesus' presence electrified the crowd. They wondered, how would Jesus heal the guy? Would He just say the word? Would He reach down and touch him? They sensed they were dancing on the edge of a miracle.

True to form, Jesus surprised them. He knelt beside the invalid and asked the strangest question in Scripture. "Do you want to get well?"

What kind of a no-brainer insult is that? Here was a man who could never run or jump or dance. He was trapped in limp and lifeless packaging, and Jesus had the audacity to ask if he might be interested in a healing.

Of course he wants to be healed . . . right?

Hold on, cowboy, maybe not.

It's a fair question. It's the same question that we must ask ourselves if we are serious about overcoming the habits that fatigue the soul. Let's get real here. Often what fuels soul fatigue is a daily diet of destructive choices. Given our decisions, we may not really want to be healed. So Jesus cuts right to the core.

> *Some time later, Jesus went up to Jerusalem for a feast of the Jews. Now there is in Jerusalem near the Sheep Gate a pool, which in Aramaic is called Bethesda and which is surrounded by five covered colonnades. Here a great number of disabled people used to lie—the blind, the lame, the paralyzed* (John 5:1-3).

The New International Version does not include verse 4, which describes the disturbing of the waters. Some manuscripts note that an angel would stir the waters and the first person to dive in after the disturbance would find healing. Ellen White comments that so great was the crowd rushing into the waters that at times weaker victims would be trampled to death in the mayhem. Ironic, isn't it? People would die in their desperate attempt to find life.

One who was there had been an invalid for thirty-eight years.

*When Jesus saw him lying there and learned that he had been in
this condition for a long time, he asked him, "Do you want to get
well?"* (John 5:5, 6).

There's the question. "Do you want to get well?"

It was a legitimate question, and Jesus did not assume the answer.
Jesus knew that some people get accustomed to their afflictions, and
they really don't want to part with them; in fact they learn how to build
a comfy life around them.

Maybe this crippled man had a system in which his infirmities served
him well. Maybe friends pampered him because of his paralysis. Perhaps they brought him food and did his laundry. Maybe he enjoyed the
freedom of not being shackled by the demands of carving out a career,
finding a spouse, and raising children. Maybe this man secretly nursed
his infirmity. After all, lounging by a pool all day isn't such a harsh
existence. Whatever the case, Jesus shoots a fair question.

A mission story comes to my mind. One morning in church I asked
if anyone had a testimony to share. My friend Kurt took the microphone.

"Last week I was driving north on Pike Street in downtown Seattle
when I passed a homeless man sleeping in an alley. He didn't have a
blanket, and it was below freezing even though the night was still young.
I couldn't shake that image in my mind." Kurt paused to collect his
escalating emotion. "I worried that he might freeze to death, so I did a
U-turn and went back to the alley. I introduced myself and learned that
his name was Ray. I told him to come home and live with me until he
could get back on his feet again, or at least until the weather got warmer.
He jumped in my car, and away we went."

Kurt went on to tell how Ray enjoyed a hot shower, a big meal, a
warm bed, a key to the house with an invitation to stay as long as he
wanted.

The irony of the story is that the man stayed for only two days, and
then he disappeared. He left a note scribbled on a paper sack. It read:
"Thanks, but I prefer to live on the streets." How could this be? Ray

had scored the jackpot. All his needs were cared for! At last, he was redeemed from the streets of crime and hate.

But who said he wanted to be redeemed? Ray preferred the life of a homeless drunk.

Now before we cast aspersions on the homeless, may I point out that many of us prefer bondage to redemption as well? Over the past decade of ministry, I have seen a steady parade of people march through my office seeking freedom from a favorite sin. The confession rings familiar: "Help!" comes the cry. "I want freedom from . . ."—and you can fill in the blank—alcohol, anger, drug abuse, masturbation, food, soap operas, romance novels, gossip, shopping, or whatever avenue of escape you prefer.

At first, I thought I could cure everybody's problems. That's because I failed to start with Jesus' question. I erroneously assumed that anybody seeking help from a pastor really wanted to be healed. More and more, however, I am discovering the rich discernment that Jesus displayed in His question of the paralytic.

Truth be told, lots of honest people have discovered that a curious kind of sadness falls over them when they consider letting go of certain character defects.

For example, most people would say, "Yes, I want to let go of my pride." But wouldn't most of us miss that rush we feel in moments of superiority? Don't we enjoy the feeling of richer than, prettier than, stronger than, smarter than, or bigger than others?

On a recent flight I got bumped up to first class. I confess that I enjoyed sitting in the oversized leather sofa while others shuffled by me into the crowded economy class. We say we want to part with our pride, but really, it feels good to be superior, doesn't it?

The curious thing about us is that often the very behavioral patterns that tend to destroy our lives are the ones we are most reticent to change. We recognize the problem with our intellect or spiritual discernment and say, "Yes, my pride is ruining my life. My anger is destroying my relationships. Gluttony is sabotaging my self-esteem." Yet we can't seem to change.

Why? That's the natural follow-up question once we have established that we really do want to get well.

Why is it so difficult to change?

First, let's acknowledge that every defect pays a dividend. We may cash in at different banks. You may frequent the bank of lust while I opt for the bank of alcoholism, but either way we give the banks the business because our defect always pays dividends. It may numb my pain. It may give me an excuse to bail. It may allow me to compensate for guilt in my life. It may get me attention. It may allow me to control other people. Whatever the case, anytime a negative behavior is repeated—even though it may be self-destructive—there is *always* a payoff.

Mother says to the kids, "Kids, come down to dinner." They don't come. So she ups the voltage in her voice and repeats, "Kids, come down to dinner." They don't come. "Kids! #@!%#@*^ Come! Down! To! Dinner!"

They come.

Mom learns that her defect of anger pays a dividend of compliance in her kids. Consequently, it is very difficult to change the defect because of the payoff.

But it's more than that. We label these character flaws or personality defects or personal challenges. These are politically correct terms for what it really is—sin. Instead of owning up, we opt for playing the victim and defending our "orientation."

Bill Leubrie commented on this bane of our culture in *The Seattle Times* in the spring of 1994.

> All women are victims. . . . One wonders how the poor, fragile dears function in daily life. All minorities are victims. Of course they are. Just ask them. No misfortune is ever their fault. . . .
>
> If you have committed a crime, no matter how horrible, you have the right to escape punishment or be punished for a lesser offense. You have the right to have your case discussed in loaded language. . . .

You see, . . . in this brave new world, we are all rudderless victims, damaged by every passing breeze. Self-determination is out. Personal strength of character is neither required nor admired. Those quaint, antique concepts are obsolete.

The new master values are whining, blame-shifting, vengeance, opportunism, and greed.

In spite of our attempts to masquerade the evil that dwells within every human spirit, the primary reason that changing self-destructive behaviors is so difficult is simply that we are wrestling against the power of sin. When Paul wonders, *Why can't I change? I do what I don't want to do and I don't do what I know I should be doing?* he answers, "because sin dwells in me."

Sin is a disease of the soul. It is a spiritual affliction, and it is progressive. You cheat on a test. Pretty soon it becomes a habit, and you rely on it to survive. Then you lie to cover up the cheating. Sin destroys the soul.

That's why James emphatically cries out, *"Therefore, get rid of all moral filth and the evil that is so prevalent"* (James 1:21). His wording describes the way a snake sheds its skin. Get rid of sin—shed it.

A graphic picture of this comes in way of a thirteen-foot snake that was the embodiment of evil. It had a scar over its left eye that prevented healthy shedding. Consequently, at least two times a year zookeepers would get the dreaded phone call from a manager in the reptile house: "The cobra shed his skin last week, but the eye cap didn't come off. We need a team to come take care of it."

I once heard about Gary Richmond, one of the zookeepers, telling of his experience. He said,

The capture of the cobra was as follows. Five of us took our positions—two keepers on either side of the cage door, the curator in front of the door, six feet away, the vet and I on either side of the curator, ten feet from the door. The keepers' only defense were sheer bird nets with two-foot handles. The door was opened. Seconds later, the king cobra appeared. As soon as it saw us, it stopped, spread its cape, and raised to full stature, so we were all looking at the snake at eye level.

Can you imagine the adrenaline rush? Think about standing within striking distance of a snake that has venom glands housing enough poison to kill one thousand adults.

The cobra trembled with excitement. With shocking quickness, it lunged at the curator—hissing and growling with malevolent rage. The skilled keepers bagged the snake's head while the curator firmly grasped its neck just behind the venom sacs. The keepers steadied the writhing body.

Gary Richmond held the snake while a colleague baited it with a carefully positioned ball of paper towels. The reptile bit down violently and began to chew. The towels dripped yellow venom. The curator passed the time with chitchat. "Did you know," he said, "that several elephants die every year from king cobra bites? A man could never survive a bite with a full load of venom. That's why we must drain the venom sacs."

According to Richmond, the trickiest part of any snake-handling procedure is in the release. He explained that more people are bitten while trying to let go of snakes than when grabbing or handling them. His final words bit my memory forever, "When it comes to snakes, they are easy to grab but hard to let go of."[1]

Sound familiar? Any snake in your life that was easy to grab but hard to let go of?

Let's face it, snakes slither everywhere in our culture. Grab a beer here and a wine cooler there, and soon you're caught in the poisonous jaws of a snake that is not so easy to drop. Or surf an adult Web site now and glance through a Playboy later and before you know it you can't seem to let go. Cheat on the chemistry quiz today then fudge on your time card at work tomorrow and in short order you are entangled by a snake of compromise that will destroy your character. All of these habits are easy to form but difficult to break.

In the beginning there was a snake in the Garden. He said to the woman before she sinned, "It's not such a bad thing. You surely won't die." So Eve latched on, and ever since the human race has struggled to let go. Now sin is a part of our nature. No wonder it is so hard to change.

Judy was a perennial patron of our church's Breathe Free Plan to Stop Smoking. For five consecutive years Judy attended. For five consecutive years she kicked the habit. But Judy was an accountant who couldn't survive the tax season without Winstons.

Judy endeared herself to our church family. She attended our parties, did our taxes, even worshipped with us on occasion. So it was a harsh slap when Judy died of lung cancer. Her doctor assured her of the inevitable consequence if she didn't stop smoking. Nevertheless, she opted for death over quitting. Why? Because Judy's struggle was more than nicotine—it was sin. And once you grab on to sin—even with two little fingers—it's very difficult to let go. Which brings up a final question.

Is healing possible?

Let's return to the story.

> *"Sir," the invalid replied, "I have no one to help me into the pool when the water is stirred. While I am trying to get in, someone else goes down ahead of me." Then Jesus said to him, "Get up! Pick up your mat and walk." At once the man was cured; he picked up his mat and walked* (John 5:7-9).

After thirty-eight years, this paralytic discovered healing in Jesus. He was unable in his own strength to maneuver himself into the water where he believed the power of healing resided. Instead, he found true healing in Jesus.

I love Ellen White's commentary on this story. She writes:

> Through the same faith we may receive spiritual healing. By sin we have been severed from the life of God. Our souls are

palsied. Of ourselves we are no more capable of living a holy life than was the impotent man capable of walking. . . . [We cry] "O wretched man that I am! Who shall deliver me from this body of death?" Let these despondent, struggling ones look up. The Savior is bending over the purchase of His blood, saying with inexpressible tenderness and pity, "Wilt thou be made whole?"[2]

There is healing in Jesus. Candie's story is a reminder of this reality.

"Excuse me, pastor." The young woman tugged on my arm in the crowded lobby after church. "I want to be baptized."

"Praise the Lord," I quipped. While her face looked familiar, I didn't even attempt her name. "That's wonderful. Um, I'm sorry, I should know you but—"

"Oh, I'm Candie. I've been coming to your church, and I would like to become a Seventh-day Adventist."

"Great! Let's hook up to make the arrangements."

Later that week I reviewed the basic doctrines of our church with her. She had studied well and was conversant in Adventist beliefs. As part of the review, I mentioned the concept of spiritual gifts. "For example," I said, "one of my gifts is teaching, so I don't mind talking in front of people."

"I think that's my gift too," she said.

"Really?" I tried to disguise my surprise. "Well then, um, would you be willing to say a few things at your baptism? Right before I baptize you, I'll ask you to share your story of how you came to Christ. Would you be comfortable with that?"

"Sure."

Sabbath morning I stood with Candie in the baptismal tank. She was prepared to tell her story. I, on the other hand, was not prepared to hear her story. I knew nothing of her background. Nor did I anticipate her testimony.

Her opening words paralyzed even the fidgets in the sanctuary. "I was a teenage prostitute and worked for twelve years as a stripper."

I had never seen the members so attentive—certainly not during any of my sermons. My pulse doubled as I wondered where her story was going next.

"My dad disappeared before I can remember him. My mom was an alcoholic. My brother is in jail. My story is smeared with sexual abuse, physical abuse, and drug abuse."

I marveled at how poised Candie could be. Her sordid saga unveiled the seediest shadows of society. Yet she spoke with rock-solid confidence and candor. I readily affirmed her intuition that she had a gift in public speaking.

"But that's all behind me now," she continued. "That old person is about to drown at the bottom of this tank. God tells me that I will rise a new creation. If God's grace can cover me, then there is no such thing in God's vocabulary as an ineligible candidate. If God can change me, He can change anybody. If God can heal me, there truly is healing for everyone at the Cross. Praise God for His incredible grace."

With that, I momentarily buried Candie and her nine-year-old daughter in Christ's death. As they came out of the water, the church members applauded for what seemed like fifteen minutes.

In that holy moment it hit me with fresh force—the power of God to forgive and transform a sinner. Only God can change a prostitute into a promise-keeper. Only Christ can reconstruct the composition of a human heart. Only He can stoop into the shadows and salvage the brokenness of a spiritual casualty like Candie. Or Carl. Or Carol.

Lest you think Candie's story is any different than yours or mine, I remind you that we are all sinners. It is only by God's miracle of mercy that we can find forgiveness and freedom from our sins. All we have to do is acknowledge His grace. Accept His gift. And arise to walk with God.

---

1. As told by John Ortberg, "A Faith That Works: No More! The Power to Stop." (M9807) Preached February 15, 1998, at Willow Creek Community Church, South Barrington, Illinois.

2. Ellen G. White, *The Desire of Ages*, 203.

CHAPTER 7

Will God Keep Forgiving Me for the Same Old Sin?

As an advice columnist for *Guide* magazine I received numerous letters similar to this one:

> Dear Pastor Karl,
> If a Christian knows he's sinning but does it over and over again, does God continue to forgive him? What does God think about this? Help me!
> A Struggler.

So how would you answer? My answer would consist of three emphatic statements.

1. There is forgiveness for that same old sin

First, consider the words of a fellow struggler who wrestled with the same question.

> *For just as through the disobedience of the one man the many were made sinners, so also through the obedience of the one man the many will be made righteous. The law was added so that the tres-*

pass might increase. But where sin increased, grace increased all the more, so that, just as sin reigned in death, so also grace might reign through righteousness to bring eternal life through Jesus Christ our Lord (Romans 5:19-21).

The apostle Paul makes it clear that through the sin of one man, namely Adam, we have all sinned. Even so, through the obedience of one man, namely Jesus Christ, there is forgiveness. Yes, even forgiveness for that same old sin that keeps creeping back into our portfolio of failures. Paul states that where that same old sin increased, grace increased even more. There is forgiveness for that same old sin.

To steal a metaphor from the world of golf, you might think of grace as a mulligan. You take a mulligan when you shank a shot out-of-bounds or dribble it off the tee and you do a rehit. You don't count the shot. You don't write it down. It won't appear on the scorecard. It will be as if it never happened. There is no record of it. No questions asked. No penalties assigned. You get to take it over again.

Wouldn't it be nice if this practice of taking mulligans could bleed into every arena of life?

You're cruising in the triple digits down Interstate 5 when you get pulled over by a police officer. When he approaches your car, however, his face softens and he tenderly says, *"Take a mulligan!"*

You haven't paid taxes in twenty years. Finally the IRS catches up with you. The auditor informs you of a million-dollar debt in back taxes and penalties. Just as you pull out your checkbook to cover the bill, the IRS agent smiles big and says, *"Take a mulligan!"*

You stay up the entire night watching Dave Letterman, Conan O'Brien, Jerry Springer, and six infomercials for the same ab machine. Your plan is to arise early to cram for the final exam. Instead, you sleep through your alarm and botch the final. You're destined to flunk the class when later that day your professor visits you with a new test that he has taken for you. You just need to sign your name. He hands you the fresh slate and lovingly says, *"Take a mulligan!"*

If you've ever been on the receiving end of a mulligan, you know it's an extraordinary thing. I will always cherish the mulligans I've received, like the one I got from Dave Benson.

I met Dave at Pacific Lutheran University while enrolled in a course called Quantitative Analysis. He was an unassuming chap who chewed on his eraser in the back row while effortlessly setting the curve for the rest of us to shoot at. That was the first of many classes we shared in our quest to permanently park the initials MBA after our names.

It wasn't until we both landed in Business Law, however, that I uncovered the true caliber of Dave's character. That's when he gave me a gift of grace that I will remember long after I forget the details of the ADA regulations and equal opportunity employment laws.

Dave and I partnered up to do an assignment that we were required to present to the class. "Let's meet early Sunday morning to work on our project," I suggested after class. "If we haul, we can knock out the whole presentation by noon."

"Sounds good to me," Dave replied.

True to form, Dave pounded on my door ten minutes early. Immediately, we started to shape a presentation worthy of a showing in Congress. With animated video and slick sound affects, we were crafting a work of art that would impress the President, not to mention the professor. That was good.

My ETA, however, was not so good. By noon, we were still tweaking the introduction. We worked feverishly against the backdrop of a TV talking to keep us company. By the end of *60 Minutes*, it seemed we still had 60 hours before the finish line. "My head is so thick," I lamented.

"Me too," Dave agreed. "Let's take one more break, then we'll come back and finish."

"No, let's just finish. All we need to do is get this stupid background color right." I growled as I manhandled the mouse in search of the perfect shade.

That's when the computer asked me a question. A *very* important question. It queried, *"Delete Bus Law ADA presentation.ppt?"* I quickly hit "Yes"—only to be asked: *"Are you sure?"*

"We don't want to save this background color, do we?" I asked. (This was in the days before computers had Recycle Bins.)

Dave OKed my opinion, and away I clicked.

No sooner did I hit the "Yes" button than the screen went blank. So did my heart.

"What happened?" Dave asked.

My eyes swelled to the size of kiwis. I couldn't talk. Never have I so desperately wanted to be wrong in my understanding of the secret rapture. *Good God,* I thought, *now would be an excellent time to take me home!* For a blurry hour we hacked, prayed, pleaded, screamed, squealed, cried, and begged the computer to give us back our twelve hours of work. My Pentium displayed the emotions of a Brillo pad. Like a professional wrestler heckling his victim, it taunted us in our pain.

Finally Dave resigned to the inevitable. "I guess we start all over."

On through the night we recreated our efforts of the day. After a dozen infomercials clattering in the background, at last we made our one-thousandth (and final) save.

Now here's the amazing thing about that whole ordeal: Dave never mentioned my mistake. He didn't blame me—although he should have. He didn't shame me—even though I deserved it. He shrugged it off as if I had misplaced a chewed-up pencil. When I insisted on wallowing in my blunder, he always replied in the same way. "No big deal," he said. "It will be better the second time."

Now *that's* a mulligan!

Can you imagine a world that's bursting with mulligans? It's hard to picture, isn't it? Our intuitive sense of justice defies the very notion of grace. That's why we struggle so with the question of whether or not God will keep forgiving us for the same sin. To give one mulligan is one thing. But to dole out a dozen mulligans on every hole, for exactly the same shank shot—why, that's ridiculous. That's scandalous. That's un-fair. That's grace.

Where sin abounds, grace much more abounds. Even though you may have fallen into the same pitfall numerous times before, there is grace for the repentant sinner. There is forgiveness for the same old sin. Once we're clear on that, we can move on to the second emphatic statement.

2. There is freedom from that same old sin

Because Paul is so definitive and clear about the scandalous scope of grace, he then plays the devil's advocate and argues with his own position. His argument follows this logic: If we are forgiven for our sin—even the same old sin—that is, if grace eclipses our sin, then why not just keep sinning? Does it follow, Paul wonders aloud, if we should then *"go on sinning so that grace may increase?"* (Romans 6:1). As emphatic as Paul was in his insistence of forgiveness, he is even more insistent about the implications of that grace. He answers in the next verse, *"By no means!"* (NIV). Other translations put it this way: *"God forbid"* (KJV); *"Of course not!"* (TLB); *"No! No!"* (NEB); *"Oh what a ghastly thought!"* (Phillips).

Paul goes on to say, *"We died to sin; how can we live in it any longer?"* (verse 2). There is no room in Pauline theology to muck around in the same patterns of sin. Instead, he speaks of a freedom from sin. Tapping into that freedom, however, requires a change of our very nature.

A friend of mine recounts his experiences while working on a garbage truck. As you can imagine, in the sweltering heat of Ohio summers the job got monotonous. One day, to break the boredom they decorated the truck. The garbage men plastered it with posters and streamers that advertised, "Just married." The problem was that no matter how much they decorated, it was still obviously a garbage truck.

Many Christians try to decorate the externals with trimmings of godliness. Unless there is a true conversion, however, it is like decorating a garbage truck. You can wear the right posters and streamers, but your nature is the same and you won't fool anybody—especially God. If you're serious about victory over that same old sin you have to change vehicles.

That's why Paul goes on in this argument with himself to say that we were baptized into Christ's death.

> *Or don't you know that all of us who were baptized into Christ Jesus were baptized into his death? We were therefore buried with him through baptism into death in order that, just as Christ was raised from the dead through the glory of the Father, we too may live a new life* (Romans 6:3,4).

The mention of baptism reflects that Paul has in mind much more than just cosmetic Christianity; this is changing a person at the very core. In Paul's culture readers understood that baptism signified a complete transformation. The word *baptize* was used to describe the practice of dying cloth. It would be immersed in the dye and come out a completely different color. Baptism was not covering up sin—it was changing the whole nature of the sinner. The ritual of baptism in that culture demanded the person cut his or her nails and hair because water had to touch every part of the body.

I recall a baptism in which I failed to completely submerge the young woman. While she was almost entirely wet, there was a section on her bangs that never got wet. She would have never noticed. Nor would anybody in the congregation have known. But I knew. And I was aware of the symbol of the complete nature of baptism. So I gave her a second hug, only this time I scooped up a handful of water and splashed it on her forehead so I could finally exhale and say, "Ahhhhh! OK!" For the record, my hang-up is biblical.

In Bible times the effect of the baptism was held to be complete regeneration; the person baptized was considered to be an infant just born. So radical was this transformation that some people believed that a man recently baptized could marry his own sister or mother because he was not just changed but a completely different person. It was the beginning of "a new life" as Paul put it. So there is not only forgiveness for sin, there is freedom from that same old sin. How does this happen? Paul goes on to explain.

If we have been united with him like this in his death, we will certainly also be united with him in his resurrection. For we know that our old self was crucified with him so that the body of sin might be done away with, that we should no longer be slaves to sin—because anyone who has died has been freed from sin (Romans 6:5-7).

Christ was crucified so that we should no longer be slaves to sin. God desperately longs to grant you freedom to live a new life in Christ. He died to give you that freedom.

Warren Bennis writes about a promising junior executive at IBM who was involved in a real risky venture for the company. He ended up losing ten million dollars for IBM as a result of a bad risk.

He was called into the office of Tom Watson Sr., who was the founder and leader of IBM for forty years, a legend in the business community. The junior executive, riddled with guilt and fear, approached Watson and said, "I guess you've called me in for my resignation. Here it is. I resign."

Watson replied, "You must be joking. I just invested ten million dollars educating you; I can't afford your resignation."[1]

Does God give up on you because you have blown it over and over? Are you kidding? He invested the life of His Son for your mistakes. He will not give up on you. Instead, He will relentlessly pursue you in order to grant forgiveness and freedom from sin. So read verse 7 again: *"Anyone who has died [in Christ] has been freed from sin."* Did you catch that? *Anyone.* Anyone means anyone—including the veteran sinners who have made a career specializing in a favorite sin.

Paul states very forcefully that we can be freed from that niche sin. How? By staying fully connected to Christ—in His death and His resurrection. As we live in the presence of Jesus, we are granted the grace to experience freedom from sin, for sin cannot coexist in the presence of God.

That's why our attempts to try and stop sinning in our own power are so futile. Sin is stronger than willpower. Freedom from sin comes not in *trying* but in *training*. Through a regimen of training disciplines (such as prayer, fasting, corporate worship, solitude, etc.) that catapult us into the presence of God, we are changed internally. Ultimately, the external guise is transformed as well.

John Ortberg's testimony rings familiar for many of us who wrestle with sin.

> For much of my life, when I heard messages about following Jesus, I thought in terms of *trying hard* to be like him. So after hearing (or preaching, for that matter) a sermon on patience on Sunday, I would wake up Monday morning determined to be a more patient person. Have you ever tried hard to be patient with a three-year-old? I have—and it generally didn't work any better than would my trying hard to run a marathon for which I had not trained. I would end up exhausted and defeated. Given the way we are prone to describe "following Jesus," it's a wonder anyone wants to do it at all.
>
> Spiritual transformation is not a matter of trying harder, but of training wisely. This is what the apostle Paul means when he encourages his young protégé Timothy to *"train* yourself in godliness."[2]

Thomas Kelly put it this way: "Don't grit your teeth and clench your fists and say, 'I will! I will!' Relax. Take hands off. Submit yourself to God. Learn to live in the passive voice—a hard saying for Americans—and let life be willed through you."[3]

3. There is a future without that same old sin

While there is forgiveness for sin, and freedom from sin, we must not ignore the final statement that flows out of Paul's letter to the Romans. There is a future without that same old sin.

In the next chapter Paul describes the agony of the battle with that same old sin.

So I find this law at work: When I want to do good, evil is right there with me. For in my inner being I delight in God's law; but I see another law at work in the members of my body, waging war against the law of my mind and making me a prisoner of the law of sin at work within my members. What a wretched man I am! Who will rescue me from this body of death? Thanks be to God—through Jesus Christ our Lord! So then, I myself in my mind am a slave to God's law, but in the sinful nature a slave to the law of sin (Romans 7:21-25).

This frustration over the same old sin leads Paul to speak of the ultimate deliverance in chapter eight.

We know that the whole creation has been groaning as in the pains of childbirth right up to the present time. Not only so, but we ourselves, who have the firstfruits of the Spirit, groan inwardly as we wait eagerly for our adoption as sons, the redemption of our bodies. For in this hope we were saved (Romans 8:22-24).

The day is coming when we will experience a world without sin. There we will find ultimate freedom from the habits and hang-ups that plague us. The struggle will subside, and we will live eternally in the physical presence of Jesus Christ!

Right now the world groans as if in the pains of childbirth, but the day is coming when there will be no more canker sores, no more cancer, no more kids in jail. The fighting in the Middle East will subside. Dictators will be unemployed. Sin will no longer saturate our world. The *National Enquirer* will be packed with stories about men who secretly enjoy dressing like men. Judge Judy can go fishing because there will be no more lawsuits. There will be lawyers, but they will have to get jobs doing useful things like making homemade ice cream—which will be nonfattening. Jerry Springer will host shows such as, "I'm secretly in love with my spouse a thousand times more than when we got married!" We will enjoy the weather of San Diego, the greens of Augusta, the tranquillity of Geneva, and the music of Nashville. The Mariners will win the pennant every year. The lion will lie down with the lamb. The dog will make peace with the rabbit. And the cat . . . will be no more! There will be no more struggle, no more sadness, and best of all, no more sin. For all people living in a saving relationship with Jesus, there is a future without sin!

So what's the answer?

How do you respond to the "Struggler" who wonders about a Christian who sins over and over again? Can God continue to forgive him?

My answer would be, "Yes! Yes! And yes!"

Yes, there is forgiveness that flows deep and red from Calvary's tree. Where sin abounds, grace much more abounds.

Yes, there is freedom from that same old sin. He who is in Christ is a new creation.

Yes, there is a future without sin. *Then I saw a new heaven and a new earth, for the first heaven and the first earth had passed away, and there was no longer any sea"* (Revelation 21:1).

---

1. Warren Bennis and Burt Nanus, *Leaders* (New York: Harper & Row, 1985), 76.

2. John Ortberg, *The Life You've Always Wanted* (Grand Rapids, Mich.: Zondervan, 1997), 47.

3. Thomas R. Kelly, *A Testament of Devotion* (San Francisco: HarperCollins, 1941, 1992), 29.

CHAPTER 8

The Gospel According to a Busted Axle

Leonard Little plays linebacker for the St. Louis Rams football team. On October 19, 1998, he got drunk and killed Susan Gutweiler in a car accident.

Susan was on her way to pick up her son from a concert. According to witnesses, she had the green light. Tragically, as she entered the intersection, a sports utility vehicle came barreling out of control, scrunching her car and stealing her life.

The man driving the Lincoln Navigator had been partying at a local club. At the time of the accident, Little had a blood-alcohol level of 0.19, nearly twice the legal limit of 0.10. He was charged with involuntary manslaughter but quickly posted bond of $25,000 and was released.

At first glance, this seems to be just another common story of stupidity in a library of tragic drunk-driving tales. Common—except this man was a professional athlete. Because of his unique skills, he was urged by the coach to suit up only days after Susan was buried. That's because in our insane world of twisted values, we wink at life so we can watch the game. After all, the game *must* go on, right?

Shortly after the accident, Rams coach Dick Vermeil publicly defended his decision to get Little back on the turf as soon as possible. " 'I'm going to treat him just like I would want someone to treat my own son,' " Vermeil said.[1] A teammate commented, " '[Little is] not a bad guy, he's not an alcoholic. It's just unfortunate that a lot of people are making him out as a bad guy, and really he's not.' "[2]

While I can't deny that Little is a nice guy, I can question the wisdom of insisting that his game must go on. Shouldn't he be nailed like any other murderer?

I think so. Lucky for Little, I'm not his judge. If I were, he would watch the rest of the season in jail. He would never drive again.

My intolerance for irresponsible drunk drivers like Leonard Little stems from a strong sense of justice. You may share my sentiment. When we talk about justice, we're simply making a case that a person should be treated as he deserves.

Now most of us do the justice thing pretty well. You slap me, and I'll slap you back. You treat me favorably, and I'll return the favor. That's justice.

In Little's case, however, he was being treated with mercy—which means he fared better than he deserved. Justice would demand that he be executed in the same way he slaughtered Susan. Mercy, on the other hand, allows him to stay in the game and rebuild his life. I suppose in my softer moments I can agree with sports reporter Mike Lopresti, who said, "There is a time for mercy, a time for understanding, a time for forgiveness. Leonard Little, by all accounts a decent man, deserves all of these."[3]

Now press the equation even further and try to grasp the concept of grace. Grace is scandalous. It's the kind of thing that causes onlookers to shake their heads and muse, "Naaaah, could never happen." Grace would put Susan's husband in jail to serve Little's sentence so that Little can play on. Just the thought makes me cringe.

And yet, that's exactly how God treats every one of us! Should God treat us with justice, every sin would result in death. Because God is merciful, however, we are spared what we deserve. Still, God stretches beyond mercy and responds to our accidents with grace. Consequently, we get far better than we deserve. *"For it is by grace you have been saved,"* the apostle Paul reminds us, *"through faith—and this not from yourselves, it is the gift of God—not by works, so that no one can boast"* (Ephesians 2:8, 9).

Grasping grace

Perhaps the most potent fertilizer for soul fatigue is our inability to grasp this concept of grace. For when we begin to understand the irrational nature of God's love, it frees the spirit to live fully. Understanding grace empowers us to buckle up and drive again.

John's gospel records the story of a disciple who failed his best friend so severely, he thought his mistake had pushed him beyond the boundaries of grace. Make no mistake, Peter had pulled some spectacular blunders in the past—the time he sank while walking on water, the time he spoke the words of Satan, the time he whacked off a soldier's ear—but nothing like the time he denied knowing Jesus. Sometimes we crash so completely that it feels irredeemable. The soul is totaled. Write it off.

What's amazing about this story, however, is that when Peter most felt the crushing burden of soul fatigue, Jesus extended the invitation to start over. Imagine Peter as he wallowed in guilt. He slumped in a boat filled with empty fishing nets. Sunrise splashed gold on the sea. Nevertheless, darkness lingered in Peter's heart. Max Lucado paints the scene:

> [Peter's] mind was in Jerusalem, reliving an anguished night.
> As the boat rocked, his memories raced:
> the clanking of the Roman guard,
> the flash of a sword and the duck of a head,
> a touch for Malchus, a rebuke for Peter,
> soldiers leading Jesus away.
> "What was I thinking?" Peter mumbled to himself as he stared at the bottom of the boat. *Why did I run?*
> Peter had run; he had turned his back on his dearest friend and run. . . . When the rooster crowed, Jesus turned. . . .

Peter would never forget that look. Though Jesus' face was already bloody and bruised, his eyes were firm and focused. They were a scalpel, laying bare Peter's heart. Though the look had lasted only a moment, it lasted forever.

And now, days later on the Sea of Galilee, the look still seared.[4]

Picture Peter, his soul overwhelmed with fatigue. His spirit raped of hope. Now, look at what happened next.

> *"I'm going out to fish," Simon Peter told them, and they said, "We'll go with you." So they went out and got into the boat, but that night they caught nothing. Early in the morning, Jesus stood on the shore, but the disciples did not realize that it was Jesus. He called out to them, "Friends, haven't you any fish?"* (John 21:3-5).

The question had a bite to it. Often Jesus' questions did. "What were you talking about on the way?" He once asked the disciples who were vying for first-class accommodations in the kingdom. "Where is your husband?" He asked the five-time divorcee. Here He asks: "Haven't you caught any fish?"

What happens next is the most unbelievable part of the story. These fishermen tell the truth about getting skunked that night. They don't offer excuses for their empty nets ("We had a 30-pounder . . . but it got away!") No, instead they admit failure. Beginnings always start with an admission of failure and the need to begin again.

> *"No," they answered. He said, "Throw your net on the right side of the boat and you will find some." When they did, they were unable to haul the net in because of the large number of fish. Then the disciple whom Jesus loved said to Peter, "It is the Lord!" As soon as Simon Peter heard him say, "It is the Lord," he wrapped his outer garment around him (for he had taken it off) and jumped into the water* (John 21:5-7).

The old Peter is coming back. He loses the trousers and dives into the water splashing toward Jesus. Maybe he recalls the last time he abandoned the boat for Jesus. On that occasion he walked on water. Of course his faith failed and he nearly drowned, but the Lord of the second chance rescued him then too.

In verse 8 the story continues:

> *The other disciples followed in the boat, towing the net full of fish, for they were not far from shore, about a hundred yards. When they landed, they saw a fire of burning coals there with fish on it, and some bread* (John 21:8, 9).

Notice how John mentions a charcoal fire. Earlier in John's gospel (chapter 18) when Peter denied his Lord he was near a charcoal fire. That fire was a symbol, a tangible reminder of the time Peter crashed and burned.

> *Jesus said to them, "Bring some of the fish you have just caught." Simon Peter climbed aboard and dragged the net ashore. It was full of large fish, 153, but even with so many the net was not torn. Jesus said to them, "Come and have breakfast"* (John 21:10-12).

Over breakfast, Jesus asked yet another penetrating question of Peter: "Do you love Me?" The first time Peter stood by the fire, he denied his Lord three times. The second time around, Peter spoke emphatically three times, only this time he stood by a fire and declared his love.

John Ortberg writes:

> Jesus says to Peter, Jesus says to everyone who's ever stood by the fire and failed God, Jesus says still to you and me whatever we've done, Get back in the game. Nurture the gifts I gave you and cherish the calling I gave you and devote yourself to the church. Feed my sheep. They need you.[5]

If you feel that you have wrecked your life beyond repair, take heart. God is a mechanic beyond belief. Ask any of Scripture's hall-of-famers, and they will testify of God's ability to get you on the road again. Ask Noah if God will forgive a drunk. Ask Abraham if God will forgive a man who sacrificed his wife's chastity because of his own cowardice. Ask Moses if God will forgive a murderer. Ask David how God responds to a man who jumps into bed with the woman next door. Ask Jeremiah if God will forgive a man drowning in self-pity. Ask Peter and he will tell you that with God, it's always possible to begin again.

Starting over

When my family moved from Virginia to the West Coast, my younger brother Paul had just landed his driver's permit. As you would expect, he was more than mildly anxious to drive.

"But Paul, we're pulling the Nimrod camper," my dad said. "It's not the same as just driving the car."

Paul, however, was convinced that he was a trucker—even had his own handle, "Flash Lightning," on the CB radio. By Kansas City the nagging reached unbearable and Dad surrendered the steering wheel— but only under strict surveillance. Over and over Dad echoed the caution, "Take it slow."

Just outside of Hammett, Idaho, Paul took the exit to refuel. He didn't notice a sign displaying the exit ramp speed so I guess he figured there was no limit. As the road curved around, however, Paul misjudged the turn and caught the camper tire on the edge of the road. He was humming at 60 mph when he overcorrected, causing the trailer to flip into the ditch.

Everybody was OK. The trailer axle, however, was irreparably damaged. The mishap translated into a two-day impromptu vacation in a one-gas-station-town that resembled Survivor Island.

Two days and hundreds of dollars later, we were ready to get on the road again. As we loaded up the car, Paul sheepishly crawled into the back seat. Dad looked at him with an incredulous expression. "Paul," he demanded, "what are you doing?"

"Um, we're, ah, ready to go, aren't we?"

"Yes," Dad said. "So what are you doing? We need to get there." With that he flipped the keys to Paul and said, "You'll have to get in the front seat to drive."

I never heard about the incident again. To this day I think of Hammett, Idaho, as a place of beginning again.

---

1. Mike Lopresti, "Rams' Little shouldn't be rushed back," *USA TODAY,* 29 October 1998, Sec. 3.

2. R.B. Falstrom, "Rams linebacker Little charged with involuntary manslaughter," *USA TODAY,* 29 October 1998, Sec. 3, 7.

3. Lopresti, "Rams' Little shouldn't be rushed back," *USA TODAY,* 29 October 1998, Sec. 3

4. Max Lucado, *He Still Moves Stones* (Dallas: Word, 1993), 135, 136.

5. John Ortberg, *Love Beyond Reason* (Grand Rapids, Mich.: Zondervan, 1998), 69.

CHAPTER 9

Digging Dirt

During wartime, there is a form of torture that has been menacingly effective. A prisoner of war is told to dig a very deep hole—one that may take days to complete. Upon completion, when the prisoner is just beginning to feel the satisfaction of a job well done, he is commanded to fill it in and start digging another hole just like it twenty feet away. When he finishes that hole he is forced to fill it in and start digging hole number three.

At first glance, you would suppose this form of punishment to be most humane. After all, the prisoner is not beaten or starved or intimidated at gunpoint. Usually he is getting good exercise and sleeping full nights. Yet psychologists inform us that it is the most effective way to drive a person clinically insane. Why?

You and I both know it is because the work serves no purpose. Tell that same prisoner to dig a five-mile drainage ditch all by himself to move sewage away from an orphanage and he could probably work for months or years to achieve that objective without going crazy. But to simply move dirt piles with no meaningful end in mind, well, it's torture in the highest order. To feel that your work is insignificant fatigues the soul like nothing else.

Through the years I have listened to the desperate testimonies of people paralyzed by soul fatigue. At the core of their complaint is the uneasy feeling that they are just moving dirt piles. I think of a depressed stockbroker who confessed to me after his retirement party, "I bought and sold stocks for thirty years. Totaling it all up, I've made millions for my clients, but now I'm not sure that multiplying their net worth was the best way I could have served those people."

Then there was the young, energetic MBA graduate who had her eyes on the president's desk. When she achieved her goal she said to me, "I've been clinging to the belief that making more money and gaining more power are synonymous with happiness. The result is a profound sense of disappointment. Why am I so bewildered and sad when my life is the embodiment of success?"

Or consider the advertising executive who said, "I put in seventy to eighty hours a week trying to get people to purchase Pepsi instead of Coke. Does it really matter?" Translation: Am I just digging dirt for no purpose?

Mark Twain, shortly before he died, wrote,

> A myriad of men are born; they labor and sweat and struggle; . . . they squabble and scold and fight; they scramble for little mean advantages over each other; age creeps upon them; infirmities follow; . . . those they love are taken from them, and the joy of life is turned to aching grief. [Death] . . . comes at last—the only unpoisoned gift earth ever had for them—and they vanish from a world where they were of no consequence, . . . a world which will lament them a day and forget them forever.[1]

When your life is over, will you vanish with no consequence? Will people lament you for a day and forget you forever? Will you fritter your life away by moving dirt? Or will you invest your life in making a difference?

I have to believe that it is the heart cry of every human spirit to do something meaningful in life. So how do you do this? To answer that question, let's consider the life of a man who made a significant difference in the history of God's people. From his life, we see three steps to help us live on purpose.

1. Follow your calling

His name was Nehemiah. After nearly 150 years of captivity and plunder for his nation of Israel, God called him to pick up a shovel and go rebuild the walls of Jerusalem. God used three primary players in this redemptive drama of His people. He called Zerubbabel—the political leader of Israel at the time. He called Ezra—the spiritual leader of Israel. Then, he called Nehemiah—a layman. Nehemiah was a servant in the court of the Persian king, Artaxerxes. But God called him to pick up a shovel and make a difference.

Nehemiah's brother reported the chaos and confusion in Jerusalem. He told of how those who survived the exile were in " *'great trouble and disgrace. The wall of Jerusalem is broken down, and its gates have been burned with fire'* " (Nehemiah 1:3). In this report, Nehemiah sensed a calling of God to do something about the travesty.

So it is with every high-impact player who makes a difference: It starts with a calling. If you want to make a difference and fulfill a noble purpose then you must follow your calling. Nehemiah was so captured by his calling that he could not eat or sleep. In verse 4 we read his words: *"When I heard these things, I sat down and wept. For some days I mourned and fasted and prayed before the God of heaven."*

When is the last time you were so moved by your mission that you broke down and cried? It's a rare person who is propelled by that kind of clear purpose. Most people I observe are hardly alive at all. In the words of C. S. Lewis, "Our age is marked by moderate vice and moderate virtue." It's not that we are so evil, but that we are so dead. The sizzle of the soul is too easily extinguished.

The poet Vachel Lindsay, in his poem "The Leaden-Eyed," describes the ennui that marks our generation:

> Let not young souls be smothered out before
> They do quaint deeds and fully flaunt their pride.
> It is the world's one crime its babes grow dull,
> Its poor are oxlike, limp, and leaden-eyed.
> Not that they starve, but starve so dreamlessly,
> Not that they sow, but that they seldom reap;
> Not that they serve, but have no gods to serve;
> Not that they die, but that they die like sheep.[2]

How many people die like sheep for lack of a personal sense of mission in life? We need Nehemiahs who are called to a purpose bigger than selfish ambition.

As George Bernard Shaw said:

> This is true joy in life, the being used for a purpose recognized by yourself as a mighty one; the being thoroughly worn out before you are thrown on the scrap heap; the being a force of nature instead of a feverish selfish little clod of ailments and grievances complaining that the world will not devote itself to making you happy.[3]

Study the story of any significant impact player, past or present, and you will uncover a sense of mission that fueled that individual to greatness. Take, for example, Dr. Martin Luther King Jr. Watch a video of him proclaiming "I have a dream," and you will see much more than a man delivering a message; you will see a missionary proclaiming his mission. To Dr. King, confronting racism was not a career; it was his calling.

Around the time of the Martin Luther King holiday, a TV commercial airs an excerpt from his famous speech. While you can't hear the words, you can read Dr. King's lips: "I have a dream." His eyes are burning with passion. His body is quivering with intensity. Every fiber in his spirit is communicating "I am a man on a mission and I will gladly die for this cause."

The first time I saw that commercial, I was moved to tears—literally. I was watching a rerun of "Love Boat" as I recall, when this commercial blindsided me. The tears tumbled. Then my wife came into the living room. She looked at me. She looked at the love boat. She could see that I was emotionally challenged . . . by a rerun of "Love Boat." She asked, "What's wrong? Did Captain Stubing get dumped?"

I quickly explained, "Have you seen that commercial of Martin Luther King?"

"Oh, yes." She understood.

There is something mysterious, almost magical, about a man or a woman on a mission. These are the mavericks who are not content to move dirt; they must make a difference.

This is not to suggest, however, that there is no downside risk or fear involved.

Whenever you get serious about pursuing your passion there will be fear. If you have no fear, then expand your dream. When your mission is so big that it terrifies you to attack it, then you're ready for the second step.

2. Swallow your fear

Perhaps this makes you feel queasy. Maybe you are afraid to attempt something great for God. After all, it's much easier to drift through life with no purpose, no calling. The downside to drifting is that fear feeds fatigue.

Nehemiah was apprehensive. The king noticed his concern and asked about it. But try as you might, you cannot hide a calling. So Nehemiah writes:

I was very much afraid, but I said to the king, "May the king live forever! Why should my face not look sad when the city where my fathers are buried lies in ruins, and its gates have been destroyed by fire?" The king said to me, "What is it you want?" Then I prayed to the God of heaven, and I answered the king, "If it pleases the king and if your servant has found favor in his sight, let him send me to the city in Judah where my fathers are buried so that I can rebuild it" (Nehemiah 2:2-5).

Even though Nehemiah was afraid, he did not ditch his dream. Instead, he swallowed his fear.

Let's face it. Most of our fears are irrational anyway. I read a survey recently that said the number one fear is public speaking. The second greatest fear is death. This always comes to mind when I am giving the homily at a funeral. It seems strange that most people would rather be in the casket than standing where I am. Doesn't that seem crazy to you?

As I reflect on my own experience, it's clear to me that the greatest payoffs in life require the greatest risk. Rarely have I regretted taking risks. Rather, it's the playing-it-safe mode that sparks the second guessing.

At my former church, one of our annual summer traditions was a trip to Wild Waves Waterpark. One summer they featured a special attraction: bungee jumping. All day the youth were hounding me.

"Karl, let's go bungee jumping," some kids from my youth group urged.

"Forget it. I'd rather chew on chalk."

"Awwww, come on. Why not?"

"Because I don't want you to dig me up in order to bury me."

"Come on, bungee jumping is safe. Nobody's ever had more than one accident."

"No way, it's not my spiritual gift."

"Hey, wait a minute," one of the kids said with a gleam. "Aren't you the pastor who just preached on how we have to swallow our fears and take risks?"

For the record, I hate it when people quote my sermons to me. They are not intended for me but for you folk. At any rate, the next thing I knew, I was on a crane heading 110 feet above a pool of water, which from that perspective looked no bigger than a glob of spittle.

To make matters worse, the attendant taping me up with Velcro was as greasy as a truck-stop skillet. I leveled with him right up front: "I don't trust you tying that strap around my ankles."

"Why not?"

"Because your shoes are untied."

When we reached the top, he said, "OK, jump."

"Whoooooaaa there, crazy cowboy," I said, "don't I get a lesson?"

"No need."

"Well, um, ah, do I jump up or down?"

"It don't matter."

"Should I keep my hands in or out?"

"It don't matter."

"Are you on drugs?"

"It don't matter." Then he explained, "I used to be on drugs, but I gave them up."

"Oh really, how long ago?"

"What time is it?" he asked with a smirk. "No really, I *used* to do drugs, but I turned over a new leaf."

Right, I thought, *then he smoked it.*

"Listen," he barked, "if you don't jump I'm pushing you." (He did have a way of being persuasive when he wanted to be.)

So in that one moment of insanity, I swallowed an ocean of fear and stepped off the platform.

I gotta tell you. I mean, I gotta tell you. It was the most exhilarating ride of my life. When my feet were safely back on earth, I wanted to hug the kids who had put me up to it and shout, "I loooooooooove you, man!"

Rarely have I regretted risks that I have taken. On the contrary, my most cherished memories are married to my biggest risks. I've discovered a simple truth: The higher the risk, the higher the reward.

The same principle rings true in the spiritual arena. David writes: *"Trust in the LORD with all your heart, and do not rely on your own insight. In all your ways acknowledge him, and he will make straight your paths"* (Proverbs 3:5, 6, NRSV). I know he's suggesting a risky plunge. To trust God completely sets you apart from the crowd. ("Come on, it won't hurt to keep the business open for one Friday night.") It exposes you to ridicule. ("Only prudes are virgins these days.") It gives you a buzz to recklessly trust that God will come through. ("You can't pay your rent; why on earth would you tithe?")

But God says "Jump, I'll catch you." If you leap, catch your breath—because you're in for the most exhilarating ride of your life!

Such was the story for Nehemiah. When he went to Jerusalem with a shovel in his hands, he signed on for the greatest adventure of his life. In no way was he about moving dirt for no purpose. He shoveled in order to change the walls. Consequently, he made a difference.

Now that's not to suggest it was easy. On the contrary, swallowing his fear only readied Nehemiah for the third step.

3. Persevere!

Rebuilding the wall was no easy undertaking for Nehemiah. Instead, construction was met with bitter resistance.

Sanballat, a Horonite, and Tobiah, an Ammonite, mocked their efforts. They claimed the Jews to be so shoddy in their workmanship that " *'if even a fox climbed up on it, he would break down their wall of stones!'* "(Nehemiah 4:3).

Not only did Nehemiah encounter great external opposition but internal harmony began to erode as well. Nehemiah's own people joined in the chorus of complaint: *"Meanwhile, the people in Judah said, 'The strength of the laborers is giving out, and there is so much rubble that we cannot rebuild the wall'* "(Nehemiah 4:10). Essentially they were moaning, "We're just moving dirt piles. We can't pull this off. What difference are we making?"

The next chapter describes how the affluent Jews were profiteering off their laboring countrymen. So Nehemiah confronts the extortion. Then Sanballat and Tobiah tried new and innovative ways to throttle the project. Nehemiah writes, *"They were scheming to harm me; so I sent messengers to them with this reply: 'I am carrying on a great project and cannot go down.' "* Nehemiah is too focused on his calling to be distracted. He continues: *" 'Why should the work stop while I leave it and go down to you?' Four times they sent me the same message, and each time I gave them the same answer"* (Nehemiah 6:2-4).

If you're serious about leveraging your life for maximum impact then you'll have to persevere. George and Alec Gallup, the famous public opinion pollsters, conducted some of the most extensive research on the qualities of success. The two men invested thousands of hours interviewing successful people in search of the common factors among all of them.

Talking with high achievers in business, the arts, literature, religion, the military, and so on, they asked questions about family background, personality, hobbies, personal values, and education. They published the results of their research in a book called *The Great American Success Story*.

The common denominator among the thousands of successful people was not extraordinary talent, or lucky breaks, or wealth. It was much simpler. Hard work. It almost seems too simple, doesn't it? Hard work!

While their answers varied widely, one common thread was woven consistently through the stories: Success wasn't something that just happened. Rather, they made it happen through focused effort and dogged determination. No shortcuts. No simple ride. No magic. No tricks. No secrets.

Success came to those willing to pay the price of hard work. The harvest of success had a direct relationship to the seeds of hard work planted. The researchers concluded: "So what we have here is an affirmation of the old-fashioned American credo that hard work and determination pay off."

Sorry, there's no magic bullet here. If you want to be successful and live on purpose, you must work hard and persevere.

Finally, we read:

> So the wall was completed…in fifty-two days. When all our enemies heard about this, all the surrounding nations were afraid and lost their self-confidence, because they realized that this work had been done with the help of our God (Nehemiah 6:15-16).

In only 52 days, God's people were elevated to an enviable position of power and respect among all nations. Nehemiah changed the world. He made a difference.

You can too! How? Follow your calling. Swallow your fear. Persevere! Your life can have purpose. Don't waste it moving dirt piles. Rather, make a difference. And while you're at it . . . change the world.

---

1. As quoted from http://www.sermonillustrations.com/a-z/p/purpose.htm, 9,10.

2. As quoted from Anthony Campolo, *Who Switched the Price Tags?* (Waco, Texas: Word, 1986), 42.

3. George Bernard Shaw, *Man and Superman*, introduction.

CHAPTER 10

Answers for Stressed-out Hound Dogs and Lambs

When I lived in Tacoma, Washington, the local newspapers created a local hero when they reported the story of Tattoo the basset hound. Tattoo never intended to go for an evening run, but had no choice when his owner shut his leash in the car door and took off for a drive—with Tattoo outside the vehicle.

Police motorcycle officer Terry Filbert was driving near North 21st and Adam Street about 7:25 P.M., when he noticed a vehicle that appeared to have something dragging from it. As Filbert passed the vehicle he saw the basset hound on a leash, "picking them up and putting them down as fast as he could."

Filbert pursued the car to a stop but not before the dog reached speeds in excess of 25 miles per hour and rolled over several times. The car's occupants, a man and a woman, jumped out when Filbert told them they were dragging a dog. The couple was distressed and began calling, "Tattoo, Tattoo!" The dog, eight months old, was uninjured, and no citation was issued.

Ever feel like Tattoo—picking them up and putting them down as fast as you can? Racing faster than you could ever run? If so, you're part of the club. These days it seems everyone is obsessed with speed.

The best-selling shampoo in America rose to the top because it combines shampoo and conditioner in one step. Heaven forbid that we would waste time with the old-fashioned rinsing we used to do. We eat at greasy hamburger joints, not because they offer good food, or cheap food, but *fast* food. In our dizzying quest to get it even faster we invented the drive-through so families could eat in minivans just as God intended.

Eugene Peterson captured it well when he wrote: "Busyness . . . is endemic to our culture. . . . Most of us have taximeters for brains, ticking away, translating time and space into money."[1]

How can we escape the tyranny of hurry? I agree with Dr. Ernest Palen, a minister of the Reformed Church of America, who writes:

> Our madly rushing, neurotic society needs therapy of silence and quietness that flows from a day kept holy, really holy. A day when our thoughts are of God, our actions are tempered by a desire to serve God and our families, a day that is so different from the other days that it could make us different in our relationships to God and to our fellow man.[2]

God never intended for His children to lead frenzied lives. Soul fatigue was never in His design. As an antidote for the hurry-sick, God crafted into the rhythm of our lives a special gift—the Sabbath. This gift dates back to the beginning of time.

> *By the seventh day God had finished the work he had been doing; so on the seventh day he rested from all his work. And God blessed the seventh day and made it holy, because on it he rested from all the work of creating that he had done* (Genesis 2:2, 3).

Now one might expect the author of Genesis to report that God finished His work on the sixth day. After all, He had completed the creation of the environment, animals, human beings, and so on. But we read that God finished His work on the seventh day.

So what did God create on the seventh day? He created the Sabbath. He made a holy day, that is, a sanctuary in time. It is a slice of eternity squeezed into earth. So God rested from His work.

Why did God rest? Clearly it was not because He was tired. He did not get to the end of Creation week and proclaim "TMIF—Thank Me It's Friday." Instead, God created a weekly season of renewal to rekindle the soul. Gordon MacDonald observes, "God subjected creation to a rhythm of rest and work that He revealed by observing the rhythm Himself, as a precedent for everyone else. In this way, He showed us the key to order in our private worlds."[3]

Ignore God's rhythm—work then rest, production then reflection, activity then ease—and you imperil your soul. Snub God's Sabbath and you will become exhausted, ungrateful, irritable, haggard, weary, and fatigued to the core. Your heart will shrink, and your spirit will become toxic. For you were created such that eternity should invade your life and breathe renewal every Sabbath. Who else knows the optimal maintenance schedule for your soul better than the Creator?

My old clunker that I drive every day reminds me of this truth. I won't say my Toyota Corolla is ancient, but the insurance on it covers fire, theft, and Indian raids. My trusty car has taken me from the General Conference in Indiana to the Grand Canyon in Arizona. For 270,000 miles now, my car has been as dependable as the Energizer bunny. I wouldn't trade it for a Mercedes Benz. (OK, I'm exaggerating now!)

Most car owners brag when the odometer eclipses 100,000 miles. I'm cruising to triple the mark and I'm still waiting for a mechanical breakdown.

So what's the secret to a quarter-of-a-million miles of trouble-free transportation?

It's simple: follow the maintenance schedule in the owner's manual. The day I drove off the car lot, I determined to follow the manufacturer's guidelines. Even though I'm as mechanically inclined as Zsa Zsa Gabor, I can do the simple stuff. Every 4,000 miles I change the oil. Every 40,000 miles I change the spark plugs. Every 10,000 miles I change the air filter. And every 1,000,000 miles I change cars!

Likewise, every human being comes with an owner's manual from the Manufacturer. God's Word gives us the Manufacturer's recommendations as to how we can best maintain our bodies.

For optimum health, it is imperative to take time for maintenance—that is, physical, emotional, and spiritual renewal. Voilá! That's what the Sabbath is all about. So important is this day of renewal that God puts it at the heart of the Ten Commandments.

> *"Remember the Sabbath day by keeping it holy. Six days you shall labor and do all your work, but the seventh day is a Sabbath to the LORD your God. On it you shall not do any work, neither you, nor your son or daughter, nor your manservant or maidservant, not your animals, nor the alien within your gates. For in six days the LORD made the heavens and the earth, the sea, and all that is in them, but he rested on the seventh day. Therefore the LORD blessed the Sabbath day and made it holy"* (Exodus 20:8-11).

Six days, God tells us, to work and labor and stress. But, on the seventh day remember to whom you belong. Remember the seed of eternity that has been planted in your heart. Remember the God who made you and loves you. Remember to hit the pause button on the dizzying hurricane of life. Remember there is rest and renewal in the arms of the Father.

In his excellent book *A Touch of Heaven*, Greg Nelson cites an intriguing experiment on the effects of stress. Using twin lambs, each lamb was placed in a pen all alone. Electrical pulsing devices were hooked up at several feeding locations in the pen. As the lamb wandered to each feeding station, the lamb sustained a burst of electrical current. Each time this happened, the lamb would twitch then race to another part of the pen. The lamb never returned to the same location once it had been shocked.

This was repeated at each feeding station until the lamb retreated to the center of the pen shaking. He had nowhere to go. Completely overwhelmed with stress, he had a nervous breakdown.

For the second part of the experiment researchers placed the lamb's twin brother in the same pen. Only this time they put his mother in the pen with him. Again, they shocked him at every feeding station. Like his twin brother, he immediately twitched and ran—only he always ran in the direction of his mother. He snuggled close to her, and she provided comfort.

She apparently reassured him because the lamb promptly returned to the exact spot where he was shocked the first time. The researchers threw the switch again. Again the lamb ran to his mother. Again she provided comfort, and again he returned to the same place.

This happened repeatedly, but as long as there was a reference point for the lamb to return to after each shock, he could handle the stress. He was able to cope.[4]

God gives you and me a vehicle through which we can cope. This reference point is the Sabbath. Amidst the shocks and anxieties of life, there is a regular retreat that our Father bids us to remember.

Rabbi Abraham Heschel alludes to this reference point:

> In the tempestuous ocean of time and toil there are islands of stillness where man may enter a harbor and reclaim his dignity. The island is the seventh day, the Sabbath, a day of detachment from things, instruments and practical affairs as well as of attachment to the spirit. . . . The seventh day is the exodus from tension, the liberation of man from his own muddiness, the installation of man as a sovereign in the world of time.[5]

So how do we remember the Sabbath day to keep it holy? Here are some suggestions.

Rest your body

> *"If you keep your feet from breaking the Sabbath and from doing as you please on my holy day, if you call the Sabbath a delight and the LORD's holy day honorable, and if you honor it by not*

going your own way and not doing as you please or speaking idle words, then you will find your joy in the LORD, and I will cause you to ride on the heights of the land and to feast on the inheritance of your father Jacob." The mouth of the LORD has spoken (Isaiah 58:13, 14).

A little girl was explaining to her younger brother that it was wrong to work on the Sabbath.

"But what about police?" asked the boy. "They have to work on the Sabbath. Don't they go to heaven?"

"Of course not," replied his sister. "They're not needed there."

While the girl may have overstated her point, the spirit of her suggestion is worth considering. Indeed, God calls us to refrain from work and school and doing as we please on His special day. He has given us this day to rest our weary bodies and recharge our worn batteries.

Render acts of service

Another time [Jesus] went into the synagogue, and a man with a shriveled hand was there. Some of them were looking for a reason to accuse Jesus, so they watched him closely to see if he would heal him on the Sabbath. Jesus said to the man with the shriveled hand, "Stand up in front of everyone." Then Jesus asked them, "Which is lawful on the Sabbath: to do good or to do evil, to save life or to kill?" But they remained silent. He looked around at them in anger and, deeply distressed at their stubborn hearts, said to the man, "Stretch out your hand." He stretched it out, and his hand was completely restored. Then the Pharisees went out and began to plot with the Herodians how they might kill Jesus (Mark 3:1-6).

Jesus' healing peeved the Pharisees because they had rules forbidding any medical work on the Sabbath except in dire emergencies. The rules even specified that substances they were normally allowed to use on Sabbath could not be taken as medicine. It was thought, for example, that a toothache could be relieved by sucking vinegar. Although taking vinegar was normally permissible on Sabbath, taking it to relieve pain was specifically forbidden.

One Rabbi told of refusing to eat an egg that had been laid on Sabbath. By his logic the hen would have worked to lay it, therefore making it impossible to eat. (Frankly I think it would have been a lot more work for the hen to hold it in all day until sundown!)

When Jesus saw the man with the withered hand he asked, "Is it lawful on the Sabbath to do good or to do harm, to save life or to kill?"

The rabbis refused to answer the question. So Jesus healed the withered hand. Thus He broke the conventional rules of Sabbath keeping. The Pharisees were so ticked that they "began to plot with the Herodians how they might kill Jesus."

Jesus challenged the whole system of rules and rituals. He showed how the Sabbath was given as a day to render acts of kindness. It was designed to be a day of joy. And what brings greater joy than to selflessly serve others? The words of E. Stanley Jones from a sermon I heard decades ago come to mind:

> The most miserable people in the world are self-centered people who don't do anything for anybody except themselves. They are centers of misery without exception. On the contrary, the happiest people are the people who deliberately take on themselves the sorrows and troubles of somebody else. Their hearts sing with a strange wild joy, automatically and with no exceptions.

I contend that Sabbath keepers ought to be the happiest people around.

Refocus your spirit

" 'There are six days when you may work, but the seventh day is a Sabbath of rest, a day of sacred assembly. You are not to do any work; wherever you live, it is a Sabbath to the LORD' " *(Leviticus 23:3).*

God tells His people that the Sabbath is a day given "to the Lord." It is a time to reconnect with our Maker.

Eugene Peterson's definition of Sabbath and Sabbath keeping would support this notion.

> *Sabbath:* uncluttered time and space to distance ourselves from the frenzy of our own activities so we can see what God has been and is doing. If we do not regularly quit work for one day a week we take ourselves far too seriously.
>
> *Sabbath keeping:* Quieting the internal noise so we hear the still small voice of our Lord. Removing the distractions of pride so we discern the presence of Christ.

What a gracious gift from the heart of our Creator! For all of us who feel like a hound dog being pulled faster than we can run, God renders relief in the Sabbath. So every week, open the present and recharge your body, mind, and soul. Reconnect with your Creator. And rest.

---

1. Eugene Peterson, *Working the Angles: The Shape of Pastoral Integrity* (Grand Rapids, Mich.: Eerdmans, 1987), 45.

2. Quoted by Greg Nelson in *A Touch of Heaven* (Nampa, Idaho: Pacific Press, 1999), 174.

3. Quoted by Nelson, 27, 28.

4. Quoted by Nelson, 171, 172.

5. Quoted by Nelson, 172.

Good and Depressed

Care to eavesdrop on a voice-mail message I just received?

Hi, Pastor Karl. I'm a dorm resident—we've met a couple times. My purpose for calling is that I need some advice, some pastoral advice if you will, on depression. I'm kinda feeling kinda lost, because of what someone's doing to me. I think I may be depressed, and I don't know what to do about it. So I figured you might be the best resource I know for getting information about it and what to do about it because I'm feeling kinda lost and I don't know what to do about it. And I want to do the right thing. Anyway, maybe a quick chat is in order. I don't know—any kind of advice. Thanks for your time.

Ironically, that's one of three messages I received just today from different people who expressed feelings of depression. Each person wanted counsel on how to deal with this dark cloud.

I haven't returned any of the calls yet, because I'm not sure what to say. I am not a therapist, psychiatrist, or counselor. I am, however, a pastor. So I'm at least qualified to share some biblical insights with someone who is blind-sided by the blues.

My favorite passage on the topic is 1 Kings 19. Read the story for yourself right now. As you read, notice three factors in depression.

The physical factor

First, there is a physical dimension to depression. Elijah was so depressed that he cried out to God, " *'Take my life; I am no better than my ancestors' "* (verse 4). Study the story and you'll discover he had just run 30 miles. He was physically wasted. So the angel's prescription for him included food, water, and sleep (verses 5-7).

If you, too, fight feelings of depression, first assess your physical needs. Are you getting enough sleep? Do you exercise regularly? Are you eating a healthy diet?

Now, I realize that habits of the taste buds are hard to lick. Onece Johnson would be the first to agree. According to the *Seattle Times*, "Onece Johnson tried hard to kick the habit. She took up smoking. She began eating laundry starch as a substitute. But the old craving still lingered."

Her addiction? Dirt. Yep, that's right, dirt.

The article reports, "Johnson has to have a daily fix of dirt, particularly her favorite, crunchy clay."

" 'I've tried to wean myself away from it,' says Johnson as she displays her soil source to visitors in her native Holmes County on the edge of the Mississippi Delta. 'On a daily average, I'd say I'd eat a tablespoonful, just enough to get a taste in my mouth, like pinching tobacco.' "

The article quotes Dr. Dennis Frate, a medical anthropologist and program director of the University of Mississippi's Rural Health Research Program, He's an authority on dirt eating and explains, " 'It's analogous to eating potato chips. A snack food is what it is.' "

Dr. Frate conducted a study, which found that one in four adult women in Holmes County ate dirt regularly. For some reason, however, the study also showed that very few men eat dirt.[1]

As a pastor, I read this article with keen interest because often we run out of food at church potlucks. Now I keep a shovel in my office. So there's always enough food—at least for the women.

Seriously, I doubt that you struggle with an obsession for dirt. But my guess is that you wrestle with some flavor of a food addiction—whether it's sugar, shrimp, or sherry. The devil knows that one of the most effective avenues to the soul is the mouth. That's why God offers so much counsel in His Word on what to eat and what to avoid.

Science confirms that there is a direct link between your food and your mood. " 'It may surprise some people to learn that many food constituents can actually affect the chemical composition of the brain,' says Richard Wurtman of the Massachusetts Institute of Technology." [2]

Frankly, I don't need some hotshot scientist to tell me that. I already know that food is a factor in soul fatigue. If I eat six bags of chips, five hamburgers, four pounds of cheesecake, three loaded pizzas, two chocolate shakes, and a partridge in a pear tree, I don't think so clearly. Double duh!

That's why God provides dietary guidelines for us to follow if we want to think and feel our best. He loaded up the Garden of Eden with everything we need to experience optimum health.

Again, modern science seconds God's motion. C. Everett Koop, former surgeon general of the United States, suggests the best menu is "a varietal diet rich in complex carbohydrates and protein obtained from whole grains, beans, peas, legumes and a selection of root vegetables. Daily servings of leafy vegetables, daily servings of fruit, a few nuts and eight to ten glasses of water."

The bottom line: Eat lots of stuff that grows in dirt. (But that doesn't mean you have to eat the dirt!)

Seventh-day Adventists have long understood this vital connection between physical health and soul fatigue. Consequently, when it comes to wellness Adventists wow the world. For example, Adventist men live 8.9 years longer than the average American man, while Adventist women outlive their counterparts by 7.5 years. Adventists rank far below the general population in the incidence of obesity, cardiovascular disease, osteoporosis, and several forms of cancer.

According to health educator Chris Rucker, "Seventh-day Adventists feel and behave decades younger than their years. They refuse to believe that aches and pains are a normal part of the aging process, nor do they believe that mental deterioration is inevitable."[3]

So why do Adventists fare so well? Rucker identifies seven health principles that Adventists uphold. Like the angel's prescription to Elijah, the principles of health may seem too elementary; but if you are serious about addressing the physical dimension of soul fatigue then you'd be well served to ruthlessly practice these seven habits.

1. Eat a hearty breakfast. Rucker reports, "Adventists stay lean and healthy by making a healthy breakfast the main meal of the day. This affords plenty of energy and brain power to get through a busy day . . . and actually promotes weight loss."

So don't skip breakfast because you're too busy or you want to lose weight. Studies show that meals consumed early in the day burn off quicker than those consumed late.

2. Nix the empty and refined calories. A stunning 89 percent of the average American diet is composed of refined foods—bleached flour, white sugar, fat, and other nutritionally useless junk. That means 1,800 calories a day do little but add flab to the waist.

3. Eat more fruits and vegetables. Fruits and vegetables are the body's best defense against disease. The suggested minimum is two servings of fruit and two servings of vegetables.

4. Eat less fat. The average American consumes 89 grams of fat per day—several times the needed amount. The best place to start cutting fat is in meats, dairy products, and fried foods.

5. Fast. Rucker advises "complete fasting between meals, as prescribed by many other health regimens." She adds, "Adventists extend the principle by following a near-fast at nighttime. . . . Many Adventists fast completely one day a week, consuming no more than water, fruit juices or herbal tea."

While you must be careful to avoid irresponsible or long-term fasting, short-term fasting can give the digestive system a rest, limit the intake of calories, and promote self-control.

6. *Exercise.* Regular exercise is not only a safeguard against obesity, but prevents all flavors of disease such as diabetes, osteoporosis, cancer, and heart disease.

7. *Reprogram your mind.* A healthy lifestyle isn't concerned only with diet and exercise. Adventists believe that wellness includes paying careful attention to forms of entertainment and recreational pursuits. It encompasses reading and video choices, amount of sleep, Bible study, prayer practices, relational issues, and a host of other influences.

It's critical to guard all avenues to the mind. Notice how the angel was quick to confront Elijah's "stinkin' thinkin'."

The mental factor

Depression gets our thinking out of whack. Elijah, feeling irrational and negative, concluded, " *'I am the only one left' "*with any loyalty to God (verses 10, 14).

That's when God gently reminded Elijah: " *'Yet I reserve seven thousand in Israel—all whose knees have not bowed down to Baal and all whose mouths have not kissed him' "*(verse 18).

Have you ever thought about the extraordinary power of attitude? Ralph Waldo Emerson once said, "A man is what he thinks about all day long." The Roman emperor Marcus Aurelius said, "A man's life is what his thoughts make of it." William James put it this way: "The greatest discovery of my generation is that human beings can alter their lives by altering their attitudes." In the Bible, we find that as a man "thinketh in his heart, so is he" (Proverbs 23:7, KJV). Therein is the power of the human mind.

Occasionally I've caught glimpses of this power. For example, during my senior year in college just before job offers were made to theology majors, I reserved a weekend to visit my parents. While I wanted to see my family, I confess that my real motive was not so altruistic. It happened that the Oregon Conference president, Elder Beck, was scheduled to preach in my dad's church that Sabbath. Since I desperately needed a job, I wondered: "What could it hurt to conveniently position myself at the dinner table and hobnob with the man who holds the fate of my future in his hands?"

As the meal unfolded, it was just as I had schemed. The atmosphere was comfortable. Conversation flowed easily. Overtures of me getting a call to the Oregon Conference were made. The meal was perfect—until dessert. That's when Mom offered a choice of blackberry or blueberry pie. I opted for blackberry while Elder Beck chose blueberry.

Now get this—my own mother thought it would be funny to substitute the whipped cream on my pie with mayonnaise. Since it looked similar, she figured it humorous to think of me squirming in front of the man that I so desperately wanted to impress.

The prank, however, backfired. I downed the dessert and never winced. Since I thought it was cream, it tasted like cream. After all, you don't expect your own mother to dollop your dessert with mayonnaise. So I gulped without a grimace—much to the bitter disappointment of Mom.

Finally, Mom couldn't stand it any longer. With everyone still at the table, she asked: "Didn't you notice anything different about the whipped cream?"

"Huh?" I responded like a perfect ditz.

"Your whipped cream," Mom continued. "We put mayonnaise on your pie instead of whipped cream."

In a rare moment of spontaneity, I quipped, "Oh! When you were in the kitchen cutting the pies I decided I wanted blueberry instead of blackberry so I swapped with Elder Beck."

You should have seen my mother's face. You should have seen Elder Beck's face. They looked liked Casper's cousins. Unfortunately, I was only fibbing. The joke really was on me. Truth is, I ate a snowball of mayonnaise and never even noticed!

"Impossible!" you say. How could that be? It's simple. It all goes back to the power of attitude. What your mind tells you is what you believe—even if you are dead wrong. That's why it is so critical to carefully guard your thinking. Believe me, I know what I'm tasting about.

In the words of Ellen White: "A contented mind, a cheerful spirit, is health to the body and strength to the soul. Nothing is so fruitful a cause of disease as depression, gloominess, and sadness."[4]

The spiritual factor

There is a final factor in Elijah's soul fatigue. He was spiritually strained as well. He tells God in no uncertain terms that he's ready to bail on the whole prophet gig. But notice God's prescription:

> *"Go out and stand on the mountain in the presence of the LORD, for the LORD is about to pass by." Then a great and powerful wind tore the mountains apart and shattered the rocks before the LORD, but the LORD was not in the wind. After the wind there was an earthquake, but the LORD was not in the earthquake. After the earthquake came a fire, but the LORD was not in the fire. And after the fire came a gentle whisper* (1 Kings 19:11, 12).

To address Elijah's depression, God came in way of a still, small voice. Often it is in what St. John of the Cross described as "the dark night of the soul" that God invades our inner worlds with a whisper. Richard Foster offers this insight:

> What is involved in entering the dark night of the soul? It may be a sense of dryness, depression, even lostness. It strips us of overdependence on the emotional life. The notion, often heard today, that such experiences can be avoided and that we should live in peace and comfort, joy and celebration, only betrays the fact that much contemporary experience is surface slush. The dark night is one of the ways God brings us to a hush, a stillness, so that He may work an inner transformation upon the soul.[5]

If darkness describes your heart, perhaps it's time to embrace the shadow. Maybe God is calling you to escape the fury and recalibrate the spirit. Jesus did this regularly. At the outset of His ministry, Jesus went to the wilderness to fast and pray. After receiving the news of John the Baptist's death, He escaped for solitude. Before choosing the disciples, He withdrew from the crowds. This pattern continued until the darkest night of His life, when He withdrew into the Garden of Gethsemane. Solitude was a regular practice in the life of our Saviour. Likewise, Jesus invites us into the same experience.

Why is solitude so important? As John Ortberg puts it, "Solitude is the one place where we can gain freedom from the forces of our society that will otherwise relentlessly mold us."[6] We live in a lethal environment, which embraces a value system that is foreign to the principles of the kingdom. So enticing are the world's notions of success, happiness, and self-worth that we can be lured into the inanity without realizing it. Thus we must withdraw on occasion.

In his book *Run With the Horses*, Eugene Peterson makes this statement:

> The puzzle is why so many people live so badly. Not so wickedly, but so inanely. Not so cruelly, but so stupidly. There's little to admire and less to imitate in the people who are prominent in our culture. We have celebrities, but not saints. Famous entertainers amuse a nation of bored insomniacs. Infamous criminals act out the aggressions of timid conformists. Petulant and spoiled athletes play games vicariously for lazy and apathetic spectators. People aimless and bored amuse themselves with trivia and trash. Neither the adventure of goodness nor the pursuit of righteousness get headlines.[7]

In solitude God hones our perspective. In a still, small voice God soothes the depressed soul. In aloneness with God we discern the despair of the world and delight in His Word, where we read the life-giving promise, *"Why are you downcast, O my soul? Why so disturbed within me? Put your hope in God, for I will yet praise him, my Savior and my God"* (Psalms 43:5).

Thomas Moore, in his book *Meditations: On the Monk Who Dwells in Daily Life,* writes:

> Withdrawal from the world is something we can, and perhaps should, do every day. It completes the movement of which entering fully into life is only one part. Just as a loaf of bread needs air in order to rise, everything we do needs an empty place in its interior. I especially enjoy such ordinary retreats from the active life as shaving, showering, reading, doing nothing, walking, listening to the radio, driving in a car. All of these activities can turn one's attention inward toward contemplation.
>
> Mundane withdrawal from the busyness of an active life can create a spirituality-without-walls, a spiritual practice that is not explicitly connected to a church or a tradition. . . .
>
> At the sight of nothing, the soul rejoices.[8]

Say what?

Well, there's my pastoral prescription for depression. Now that I've got it written out, I think I'll return three phone calls. I finally know what I'm going to say.

1. Kathy Eyre, "Oral History," Seattle *Times,* 18 Dec. 1988, X.
2. "Food & Mood," *Nutrition Action Health Letter,* Sept. 1992, 1.
3. Chris Rucker, "Why Seventh-day Adventists Live Longer," *The Bottom Line,* 15 October 1991.
4. Ellen White, *Medical Ministry,* 106.
5. Richard Foster, *Celebration of Discipline* (San Francisco: Harper & Row, 1978), 90.
6. Ortberg, *The Life You've Always Wanted,* 90.
7. Eugene O. Peterson, as quoted in *Bible Illustrator,* Parsons Technology, X.
8. Thomas Moore, *Meditations: On the Monk Who Dwells in Daily Life* (New York: HarperCollins, 1994), 4.

CHAPTER 12

The Party or the Porch?

A teacher was telling the story of the prodigal son to her Kindergarten class. She described the excitement the family felt at the son's return. But then, thinking about the older brother, she said, "But there was one family member for whom the return of the prodigal son brought no joy or celebration. Someone experienced only anger, disappointment, and grief. Who was that?"

One kid piped up, "The fatted calf."

Now, I don't mean to brag here, but I would have aced the quiz. Why? Because of all the characters in Scripture, that older brother is the one I most readily identify with. Many times I have felt his angry, complaining, condemning heart in me.

Just last week nightmares harassed my daughter, Lindsey, which jolted awake both my wife, Cherié, and me. Eventually, Cherié and Lindsey drifted back to sleep. But it wasn't so easy for me. I churned and fumed. Finally, I faced the fact that I would be attacking a full day of meetings on three hours of rest.

Rather than quietly slipping out of the bedroom, however, I went on a noisy rampage as I got dressed. Somehow it didn't seem fair that they should sleep if I couldn't. Ugly words were exchanged.

"Be quiet," Cherié snapped. "You're going to wake Lindsey."

"And what do you care? You both can sleep all day. I have to go to work."

The quarrel only got uglier. I was so hot that I refused to talk to Cherié for several days.

Now why would I do that? Because I suffer from a heart condition known as EBS—Elder Brother Syndrome. It is a telltale symptom of soul fatigue.

The poster child for EBS is the older brother in the well-worn parable of Luke 15. Before we meet the brothers, notice what prompted Jesus to tell the story. Only then can you appreciate the raw boldness of Jesus as a storyteller. There is great drama in the parable when you consider the context.

"Now the tax collectors and 'sinners' were all gathering around to hear him. But the Pharisees and the teachers of the law muttered, 'This man welcomes sinners and eats with them'" (Luke 15:1, 2).

Jesus put the religious snoots on tilt because He insisted on hanging out with spiritual zeroes. In their minds, these sinners didn't really matter to God.

Now before we *tsk tsk* at the Pharisees, let's admit that many of us carry similar lists of people we believe don't matter much to God.

Chauvinists don't think women matter to God.

Racists don't reckon that minorities matter to God.

Some Christians don't think Muslims matter to God.

Occasionally, I catch a peek at my unpublished list. This happened the time I attended what sports commentators dubbed "the hockey game of the decade." The Russians were once again pitted against the Cinderella Yankees in the gold medal round of the Goodwill Games.

You can only imagine my excitement when a buddy informed me that he snagged us some complimentary "VIP" tickets for the big game! That meant free parking, free brunch, and seats so close to the ice you could feel a twinge of frostbite.

The game lived up to its billing—and then some. With one minute left, USA was up by one. The victory seemed so sure, the guy sitting next to me left in an attempt to beat the crowd. Other frenzied fans pressed against the glass ready to storm onto the ice.

With ten seconds remaining, thousands of fans screamed, "Ten, nine, eight, . . ."

Then with three seconds to play, some Russian uncorked a slap shot that launched the puck into the upper corner of the net. In shock, fans drifted back to their seats to wait for overtime.

That's when I noticed the seat next to me was once again occupied. Only this time some kid sat there.

"Excuse me," I snipped. "Is that your seat?"

Of course I knew it wasn't. "This is the VIP section, you know," I said, my elitist spirit leaking like poison.

"I want to sit here," the kid replied with an accent. "I just want to say something to my dad."

"Dad? Who's your dad?"

"He's the coach for the Russian team. He's right there, wearing the red tie."

"Right!" I scoffed. "And my dad is Boris Yeltsin."

Although skeptical at first, after seeing him and his dad communicate for a while I concluded that indeed this kid was who he claimed to be.

Soon, all the people around us picked up on the kid's identity. Suddenly, nobody wanted to see him leave. Hockey fans fired questions at him like an interrogation machine gun. "What is life in Russia like? Who is your favorite player on the Russian team? What is it like to travel with the team?"

Finally, I wanted to say to the nosy needlers, "Quit with the questions, and leave the kid alone. Let us talk. He's *my* friend."

The game ended as everyone expected. Russia mined the gold, and we went home disappointed. But my greatest disappointment about the game came later, when I reflected on how I treated the coach's kid.

I wrote in my journal: "I treated that kid entirely different once I discovered who he was. I'm embarrassed to admit that when he was a 'nobody' in my mind, I had no time for him. When I saw him as the coach's son, suddenly I buddied up like a boozer to a bottle. How sick."

Then James's punchy words came to mind:

> *Never think some people are more important than others. Suppose someone comes into your church meeting wearing nice clothes and a gold ring. At the same time a poor person comes in wearing old, dirty clothes. You show special attention to the one wearing nice clothes and say, "Please, sit here in this good seat." But you say to the poor person, "Stand over there," or, "Sit on the floor by my feet." What are you doing? You are making some people more important than others* (James 2:1-4, NCV).

Pretty clear, isn't it? In the church of Christ, there is no room for elitism. Jesus felt so strongly about this that He told three stories back to back to back in order to teach a simple truth—*all* people matter to the Father.

You probably know the stories. A shepherd loses one of a hundred sheep, and since that one sheep matters to the shepherd, he pursues it.

In the next story a woman loses a coin, and since that coin matters to her, she goes after it.

Finally, a father loses a son, and that son matters deeply to the father.

To the religious grumblers Jesus is saying, "Not only do I not apologize for accepting these people, I tell you flat out that what you see is the work of God."

Now, that would have been dramatic enough, but Jesus kept preaching. He really turns up the heat when He introduces another character into the third story.

"Meanwhile, the older son was in the field. When he came near the house, he heard music and dancing. So he called one of the servants and asked him what was going on. 'Your brother has come,' he replied, 'and your father has killed the fattened calf because he has him back safe and sound.'

The older brother became angry and refused to go in. So his father went out and pleaded with him" (Luke 15:25-27).

An angry heart

The first symptom of EBS is anger. There's a party going on. Every one in the village is there. But the son refuses to participate.

This is more offensive to Jesus' listeners than we might realize. As the oldest son, he would have a duty to co-host with the father at a public gathering like this. In that culture it was an obligation of the first-born.

The listeners knew that snubbing an invitation to a family festival was a serious offense. Remember the story of Esther, when Queen Vashti, the king's queen, refused to attend a banquet when he called her? She was deposed.

So the brother's refusal to celebrate was a highly dramatic action to Jesus' listeners. The kid deliberately wanted to expose his father to public humiliation. Everybody would gossip about the boy's brazen behavior. They would expect the father to be furious. He had every right to explode. He could have demanded that the son go into the house. No doubt the son would have obeyed. Instead, the father tries to lovingly reason with the rebel.

Still the son would not go in. Instead, he revels in his resentment. He likes torturing himself, sitting on the front porch, listening to the music but not going inside. It feeds his sense of self-righteous virtue. It gives him control. It justifies his anger.

I once heard a pastor explain it this way: "Of the seven deadly sins, anger is the most fun. To lick your wounds, to smack your lips over grievances long past. . . . In many ways it is a feast fit for a king. The chief drawback is, what you are wolfing down is yourself."[2]

Perhaps you're sitting on the porch right now. You have a parent who did not meet all your needs. Or a roommate who wounded you. Or a neighbor who slandered you. You're enjoying the anger. It's feeding your sense of self-righteous superiority. The problem is, holding on to anger is like swallowing poison and hoping the other person will die.

Meanwhile, there is a party going on. It is composed of people who have discovered the joy of releasing their anger and reveling in the forgiving fellowship of family.

A complaining heart

Another symptom of EBS is a spirit of complaint. *" 'But he answered his father, "Look! All these years I've been slaving for you and never disobeyed your orders. Yet you never gave me even a young goat so I could celebrate with my friends" ' "* (Luke 15:29).

When Jesus told the story his listeners would have been shocked at the son's disrespect. Notice that he would not address his dad as "father." Titles of respect were taken very seriously. Even the prodigal son had the decency to address his father with the appropriate title. But the older son breaches all common etiquette and just launches into his complaint.

" ' "All these years" ' " he whines, *" ' "I've been slaving for you and never disobeyed your orders." ' "* His words ring with such irony. He claims perfect obedience right after he publicly defies his father. Furthermore, he identifies himself as a family slave. The prodigal son begged to be taken back as a slave, but when he found himself in the father's loving embrace he immediately nixed that notion and was reinstated as a son. The older brother stayed home, but he was never really a son, but rather a slave. That's because he sees himself as a victim. He opts to soak in his sorrow rather than prance into the party.

Still today, there is a party going on. It is composed of people who choose joy over complaint. So how's your heart on this one?

I once heard Tony Campolo share the following story:

Years ago I took my son to Disneyland when he was just a little tyke. This was back in the days when you had the tickets for the rides. Now you have this huge general admission and you don't get on the rides anyway. But you had the tickets, remember the tickets?

We were leaving Disneyland at 9 o' clock and my son said, "I want one more ride on Space Mountain."

I said, "We're out of tickets, son, and I'm out of time."

He said, "But Jesus wants me to go."

I was intrigued with his answer.

He said, "Sunday when you were preaching, you said every time we cry Jesus cries because He feels everything we feel. Well if He feels *every* thing we feel, then when I'm laughing and having a good time, He feels it. He would enjoy me having one more ride on Space Mountain."[3]

Now, that's not bad theology. The truth is, God created us for joy. Check out Genesis 1 and 2 for yourself. You will discover the heartbeat of the Creation story is joy. The whole story throbs with the refrain "God said, . . . And it was so . . . and indeed, it was very good."

You can try to read a sour spirit into our Creator, but you won't find it. Rather, all of creation expresses God's joy. Listen to how the psalmist describes the sun: *"It bursts forth like a radiant bridegroom after his wedding. It rejoices like a great athlete eager to run the race"* (Psalms 19:5, NLT). Pastor John Ortberg comments,

> This is not merely picturesque language; this is creation expressing God's own unwearying joy at simply being, at existing and knowing existence to be good. As products of God's creation, creatures made in his image, we are to reflect God's fierce joy in life.[4]

That's right. For the Christian, joy is not an option—it's a command. *"Be full of joy in the Lord always,"* the apostle Paul wrote. *"I will say again, be full of joy"* (Philippians 4:4, NCV).

The older brother knew nothing of this joy. Instead, he bled complaint.

Condemnation

The third symptom of EBS is condemnation. The older brother's tirade continues: " ' "*But when this son of yours who has squandered your property with prostitutes comes home, you kill the fattened calf for him!*" ' " (Luke 15:30).

Notice how he dehumanizes the younger brother by referring to him as "this son of yours." He doesn't use his brother's name. Nor will he acknowledge him as a brother.

Also notice that it's the older brother who mentions prostitutes. Where did that come from? Jesus never mentioned the detail. The older brother throws it in to paint his brother in the most unsavory colors possible. He is quick to condemn.

There is a party going on. It is composed of people who live out the command of Jesus, " '*Do not judge, or you too will be judged*' "(Matthew 7:1). When I adopt a judgmental attitude it's easy to forget that I am just a flawed and fallen human being. I assume a position of superiority and set myself up for a fall.

Don Shula, the long-time coach of the Miami Dolphins, tells a wonderful story about this. Vacationing in a small town in Maine, he commented to his wife on how difficult it was to escape the accolades and recognition from fans. Walking into a movie theater, the handful of people present exploded in applause. "See," Shula grinned to his wife, "I guess there is no where in the world we can go where people don't recognize me."

After finding a seat Shula shook hands with the guy next to him. "I am surprised you recognized me," he said with a blush.

The guy studied Shula's face. "Am I supposed to know you? We were just glad you came in because the manager said he wasn't going to show the movie unless there were at least ten people here."

I think we all need these reminders to keep us humble. Humility is the antidote for EBS. It is the recognition that we all possess a part of the prodigal. We have all wandered from the Father. Everyone needs grace.

How are you feeling?

It's time for a check-up. Recognize any symptoms of EBS in your soul? If so, pay careful attention to the father's reaction. " ' "*My son,*" the *father said, "you are always with me, and everything I have is yours. But we had to celebrate and be glad, because this brother of yours was dead and is alive again; he was lost and is found" ' "* (Luke 15:31, 32).

The father overlooks all the insults that his son has leveled at him. Even though his son did not address him as Father, he shows respect and addresses the boy as "my son."

It's significant to note that this is not the usual Greek word for son. The father uses the word *teknon*, which was the word used to address a little child. It is a very tender word. "My child," the father says to the boy who wouldn't call him Father, "you are always with me, and everything I have is yours."

The father is saying, "Your brother took his portion, so everything left is yours. But the real inheritance blessing is that you have been at home with me, to live in my love, to share all things with me, to partner together throughout life, . . . these are the greatest gifts."

If living at home with the father is not enough then all the property in the world will fail to satisfy the searching of the soul. The father is infinitely gracious with this son, yet tenaciously firm. He will not apologize. Nor will he squash the party. That's what the older son wants. He wants Dad to feel bad and silence the singing. But the elder son is not allowed that kind of power.

Imagine Jesus' listeners. Some of them are bursting with joy, because they identify with the prodigal and exclaim, "That's me. But now I can come home, and that is cause for God to throw a party." Others are burning with anger, because they identify with the older brother. They feel the indictment of God's words.

At the pinnacle of drama in the story, Jesus does the most amazing thing. He stops talking. He never finishes the story. Why? Well, it's not because He couldn't think of an ending. Rather, it's because the ending had yet to be written.

The story would end one of two ways. The older brother could turn away from his father, return to the field, and work with a cold and bitter heart until the day he died of EBS. Or he could enter the house and laugh louder, sing longer, dance faster, and cry harder than all the other party animals. For he, like everyone else at the celebration, was granted astonishing grace from the heart of the father.

How does the story end? It's up to you.

I can tell you how the story ended for me. After camping in this parable for days, the question kept badgering me: The party or the porch? For days I stewed in my anger, convicted of my "rightness" while condemning Cherie's obduracy.

But the EBS was killing my spirit and fatiguing my soul. It always will.

Well, I finally decided to join the party myself. I did something that does not come naturally to me. I said to Cherie, "I'm sorry for my hateful and hurtful words the other night. I'm sorry I have been ignoring you because of my anger. Can you forgive me?"

Graciously, Cherie allowed the fractured friendship to heal. And once again I was reminded that living in the party is just a better way to do life.

So where are you going to live? The party? Or the porch? It's up to you.

---

1. I am indebted for the inspiration of this chapter to John Ortberg's sermon: "Love for the Bitter Heart" (C9819) (South Barrington, Illinois: Seeds Tape Ministry, a ministry of Willow Creek Community Church, 1998).

2. John Ortberg quoting Frederick Buechner in "Love for the Bitter Heart."

3. Tony Campolo, in a speech addressing employees of the Adventist Health System, 1999 Conference on Missions in Orlando, Florida.

4. Ortberg, *The Life You've Always Wanted*, 67.

CHAPTER 13

Living Above the Drip

Drip. Drip. Drip. Drip.

The demands on my life are no less insistent than when we began this journey. Yet through the seasons of inner fatigue, I have discovered three guiding principles that anchor the soul and allow one to live above the drip. Make these moorings your mantra and you too can endure the darkness with an underlying sense of serenity. Compromise here, and you sabotage your soul. So pay careful attention to the counsel of the apostle Peter, who gives us a sure strategy for addressing soul fatigue.

Live with nothing to hide

"But just as he who called you is holy, so be holy in all you do; for it is written: 'Be holy, because I am holy' " (1 Peter 1:15, 16).

Peter's first challenge is to holiness. Issues of the soul are entwined in matters of integrity. To live with nothing to hide is to enjoy a freedom of the spirit. In the words of Johann Tauler, "True peace is found by man in the depths of his own heart, the dwelling-place of God."[1]

This sense of true peace can come in the most unlikely places. For example, I felt this peace at a ticket counter once. I was talking with an agent who acted like a Rottweiler that hadn't been walked for a week.

"I'm sorry sir, but you can't take that as a carry-on bag," she growled as she pointed at my garment bag.

"But I called before coming to the airport," I protested. "And your airline representative said I could carry on one garment bag."

"Yes, but your garment bag is overweight and oversized. And you've already reached your allowance for checked baggage. You'll have to leave your garment bag here—or pay the fee for an extra piece of baggage," she ordered. "Whatever you do, get out of the way. You have a lot of people waiting behind you, and we are understaffed today."

I knew I really had no choice. I was leaving as a student missionary for the year, so I needed the garment bag. And because I was by myself I couldn't send it home with somebody.

"OK," I sighed, "how much will it cost to bring this extra baggage?"

"One hundred and twenty dollars."

I pealed off the traveler's checks like a starving ape surrendering bananas. *Great!* I thought. *Now I only have eighty dollars to last me all the way to South Africa.*

Later, when flipping through my traveler's checks, I counted one hundred dollars. I wanted to believe that God was doing a multiplication trick as He did with the loaves and fishes. But I couldn't escape the truth that I had underpaid Ms. Rottweiler by $20.

That's when the mind wars began. *After the way she treated me,* I reasoned, *she deserves to be cheated. God is teaching her a lesson. Keep the dough.*

That thought, however, couldn't reign uncontested. My conscience argued back. *What would Jesus do? How can He bless you as a student missionary if you are a thief? Go pay it.*

Back and forth the voices dueled. The sticky strands of guilt entangled me like a cobweb soaked in superglue. I knew peace would be hard to come by if I didn't do the right thing.

"Excuse me, ma'am," I said as I returned to the counter.

"What do you want this time?" she snapped.

"I counted my traveler's checks and realized I underpaid you."

"I filed your checks in the back. I'm sure you paid the right amount. I can count, you know."

"Very well," I sighed, "but I'm sure I owe you twenty dollars."

"OK, OK," she huffed. "I'll go get your money and show you."

Upon retrieving the checks, she started counting in front of me—as if to humiliate me in the process. "Twenty, forty, sixty, eighty, one hundred." Then confusion covered her face, and she began to count the checks again. Suddenly she snapped up the check I was holding out for her. "Some people are impossible!" she snipped.

"Ma'am, I was thinking the same thing." (Sorry, I couldn't resist.)

I left the ticket counter without so much as a simple "Thank you" from her. But I knew I had done the right thing. I was $20 poorer, but I had a sense of peace worth millions.

That's what God desires for every one of His children—peace. And there's no better way to obtain that peace than to live with nothing to hide—even if it costs you.

Live with nothing to prove

The second principle calls us to live in the security of God's love. Peter continues:

> Since you call on a Father who judges each man's work impartially, live your lives as strangers here in reverent fear. For you know that it was not with perishable things such as silver or gold that you were redeemed from the empty way of life handed down to you from your forefathers, but with the precious blood of Christ, a lamb without blemish or defect (1 Peter 1:17-19).

This passage always reminds me of Kevin Costner and a restroom. I'd better explain that. Recently I attended a game at The Forum to watch the Los Angeles Lakers host the New York Knicks. At half-time my brother, Paul, and I were moseying toward center court when we spotted Kevin Costner. We gawked at the Hollywood superstar sitting no more than 20 feet away.

"Let's see if we can't get a little closer," I said with a gleam in my eye.

"Great idea," Paul agreed.

Suddenly Costner got up and headed for a roped-off area on the main floor. Galloping toward a posse of security officers, I whispered to Paul, "Just follow him into that room. Act like we know where we are going and the security officers will never know. And don't look at anybody."

We eased into the restricted area like FBI agents at a crime scene. We slid through a tunnel of tinsel created by the Lakers' dance team and on through a stately, mahogany door—into a restroom.

That's when my slimy nature hit me upside the soul. *Here I am*, I thought, *a grown man, a pastor, 34 years old, jockeying for a better view of another grown man standing in the restroom. How sick is that?* Then I wondered if I was breaking a law. (On second thought I reasoned, no—after all, I was in California!)

But I have to admit that in that context Kevin Costner looked *very* human. The truth suddenly hit me: Kevin Costner is no different than you or me. The big screen persona disappeared. That's because the picture that Hollywood paints of success is a mirage. Supermodel Cindy Crawford said it well when she quipped, "The Cindy you see in the magazines and on TV is not me. I'm not sure who she is but it's not me." Hollywood promotes what Peter dubbed "an empty way of life."

It is a sad commentary that so many people live from childhood to retirement trying to prove their worth via the empty way of the world.

Some find their value in *performance* . . .

"I landed the largest contract in the history of our corporation."

"I am a scratch golfer."

"I sing like Celine Dion."
Some find their value in *possessions* . . .
"I drive a BMW."
"My portfolio is worth over a million dollars."
"I've got the top-of-the-line snowboard."
Still others find their value in *position* . . .
"My degree is from Harvard University."
"I am the youngest senior vice-president in the history of the company."
"I have over a thousand people working under me."

According to Peter, we don't need to prove our worth here; we're strangers in this world. We embrace a different value system. We don't keep score the same way. Our worth does not come in silver or gold or boats or sports cars or homes, but our value is rooted in *"the precious blood of Christ, a lamb without blemish or defect"* (1 Peter 1:18).

This makes sense when you think about what determines value in the first place. What makes something valuable?

Barbra Streisand once sold a few of her valuables. She explained, "I want only two houses, rather than seven . . . I feel like letting go of things." (Tsk, tsk, poor darling; how will she survive with only *two* homes?) So she sent her Tiffany cobweb lamp to the auction—and fetched a cool $717,500. What, pray tell, makes that lamp any more valuable than the K-Mart special that sits on my desk? My lamp shines as bright as hers. Why is mine worth $6 and hers worth a corner of Fort Knox?

What determines value?

Value is determined by what somebody is willing to pay for it. At the same auction, Streisand sold a nude painting of Adam and Eve for nearly $2 million. What makes the painting so valuable? That's what somebody coughed up for it.

Recently, some neighbors held a garage sale. The following day I asked how it went.

"It was incredible!" my neighbor beamed. "By noon we had sold about everything on the tables—which sent us scrambling through the house in search of more junk to sell. That's when I happened upon an old macramé owl. It was tattered and one eye was missing. Feeling embarrassed to display it, I marked it 25 cents and put it on the back of the table."

"Did it sell?" I asked.

"That afternoon, two women spotted it at the same time. The first lady said, 'I'll buy that owl.'

"The second lady protested, 'I saw it first, I'm buying it.'

" 'I'll pay 50 cents' snipped the first lady.

" 'Seventy-five cents,' countered the second.

" 'One dollar!'

" 'Two dollars!'

Do you know what the owl sold for? . . . One million dollars!

I'm kidding, of course (that's the way the story is supposed to end). It did, however, sell for 10 times it's original price. Why? Because some clutteraholic invested two and a half bucks—which means it's worth $2.50. (I wouldn't have paid Monopoly money for it.)

In the same way, your value is not determined by your performance, possessions, or position. Rather, your value is anchored in what God was willing to pay for you at Calvary. When this truth settles deep within you, you are empowered to live with nothing to prove.

Live with nothing to gain

A final principle that combats soul fatigue is to live with nothing to gain. *"Now that you have purified yourselves by obeying the truth so that you have sincere love for your brothers, love one another deeply, from the heart"* (1 Peter 1:22).

What would happen if we really lived that verse? What if we loved one another deeply, from the heart? What if we served recklessly, with nothing to gain? In the final analysis, I think that's the most important thing we could do.

The apostle Paul said as much in 1 Corinthians 13. Here's the familiar passage from the KHV (Karl Haffner Version):

If I speak with the confidence of Rush Limbaugh and sing with the ease of Pavarotti, but don't have love, my words are like scraping fingernails on a frozen windshield. If I can program NASA's mainframe computer or outsmart my chemistry professor, if I memorize the Psalms and read Leviticus without dozing, or if I can even predict the future . . . but have not love, my value is equal to a pitcher of warm spit. If I give my Tommy Hilfiger wardrobe to Goodwill and let my little sister rummage through my closet, if I go to the stake and fry as a martyr, or if I donate a gallon of blood every hour, but don't love, my offerings are useless.

Love is patient—even if it means skipping a trip to 31 Flavors in order to tutor an immigrant. Love is kind—it doesn't stoop to Polish jokes, Whitey jibes, slanty-eye stories or jokes about Jews. Love does not envy the president of the company, the National Merit finalist, the model mom with quiet kids, or even the blond who sports the world's most even tan. Love isn't snooty about a new Corvette or a season pass to the world's premiere ski resort. Love never jeers the fat kid who hangs out of her T-shirt in PE. Love smiles at getting cut off on the interstate. Love submits an honest tax return. Love doesn't whine about the referee's bad call. Love believes that God always provides the best stuff in life. Love hangs on to hope when the family is splitting apart.

Love does not change like hemlines and hairdos. Love is like the Energizer bunny. It lasts and lasts and keeps on going. In the end only three things will remain: faith, hope and love. But the greatest of these is love.

So what are we waiting for? Let's spill out our lives in reckless service to others.

The drip is back

Drip. Drip. Drip. Drip.

The taunting noise of life keeps clamoring for our attention. Who has time to think deeply about matters of the soul when the drip feels so demanding?

Focus on that drip, however, and it will eventually rub the soul raw. The drip can be so distracting that we miss the whole adventure of God. He created us to live in the spirit of the kingdom. How? Live with nothing to hide, nothing to prove, and nothing to gain. It is the secret of the kingdom, hidden in plain sight.

---

1. Edythe Draper, *Draper's Book of Quotations for the Christian World* (Wheaton: Tyndale, 1992), #8474.

If you enjoyed this book, you'll enjoy these as well:

Devotional Retreats
Debbonnaire Kovacs. Refresh your spirit and draw closer to Jesus than you ever dreamed possible through *Devotional Retreats*—a method of using your five senses to meditate on scripture making the stories of the Bible spring to life in your own imagination.
0-8163-1837-9. US$10.99, Can$16.49.

Escape to God
Jim Hohnberger with Tim and Julie Canuteson. The true story of how a prosperous Adventist family left everything behind to live in the wilderness and find genuine spirituality and the simple life.
0-8163-1805-0. US$13.99, Can$20.99.

5 Steps to Christlike Living
Randy Maxwell. Topics on everything from how to know God's will in your life, to how to live with an unbelieving spouse are addressed with candor, wit, and in Randy's popular "Five Ways" format. Use alone or in small groups.
0-8163-1816-6. US$9.99, Cdn$14.99.

Order from your ABC by calling **1-800-765-6955**, or get online and shop our virtual store at **http://www.adventistbookcenter.com.**

- •Read a chapter from your favorite book
- •Order online
- •Sign up for email notices on new products

Prices subject to change without notice.